Arts & Crafts

Steven Adams

SILVERDALE BOOKS

A QUANTUM BOOK

This edition published by Silverdale Books,
an imprint of Bookmart Ltd., in 2005
Blaby Road
Wigston
Leicester
LE18 4SE

Copyright © 1987 Quintet Publishing Ltd

This edition printed 2005

ISBN 1-84509-226-0

QUMA&C

This book was produced
by Quantum Books Ltd
6 Blundell Street
London N7 9BH

Printed in Singapore by
Star Standard Industries Pte Ltd.

CONTENTS

INTRODUCTION

Portrait of William Morris. Morris was a cornerstone of the Arts and Crafts Movement. A designer of books, typefaces, fabrics and furniture, as well as a prolific writer on both art and politics, Morris was among the first to give practical form to the Utopian ideals of Carlyle and Ruskin.

The Arts and Crafts Movement evolved and developed during the second half of the 19th century. It incorporated a wide variety of artists, writers, craftsmen and women, so wide that it is difficult to define 'Arts & Crafts' with any accuracy. One has only to consider that some of its precursors were deeply conservative and looked wistfully back to a medieval past, while others were socialists and ardent reformers. Some, like John Ruskin (1819–1900), identified the Arts and Crafts aesthetic with Protestantism, while others, such as the architect Augustus Welby Pugin (1812–52), saw clear affinities between the revival of medievalism and the Catholic cause. Moreover, the craftsmen and women connected with the movement were active within a wide cross-section of crafts: as architects, printers and bookbinders, potters, jewellers, painters, sculptors, and cabinetmakers. Some members of the movement, such as the designers William Morris (1834–96) and C.R. Ashbee (1863–1942), cherished handicraft and tended to reject the opportunity to produce for a mass market. Others, such as the architect Frank Lloyd Wright (1867–1959), positively relished the creative and social advantages of machine production.

The Arts and Crafts Movement became even more diverse in the 1870s, when the revival of an interest in the Arts and Crafts in Britain was exported and grafted onto indigenous traditions abroad. In the United States, the revival of craft traditions had a resonant appeal for a nation with a strong political affinity with individualism and for things handmade and homespun. It is interesting to note that decades before critics such as Thomas Carlyle (1795–1881) or Ruskin were writing about the horror of industrialism and the idyll of rural medieval England, Shaker communities in the United States were producing simple furniture and buildings that echoed many of the creative and social ideals of the Arts and Crafts Movement. Friedrich Engels (1820–95) dissociated himself from the religious faith of the Shakers but admired the near-socialist conditions under which their work was produced and sold.

The revival of Arts and Crafts in the second half of the 19th century embodied a rich and varied tradition of political, religious and aesthetic ideas that found form in a variety of media, yet there were some principles and articles of faith common to the Arts and Crafts Movement in general. The belief that a well-designed environment – fashioned with beautiful and well-crafted buildings, furniture, tapestries and ceramics – would serve to improve the fabric of society for both producers and consumers is a theme common to the Arts and Crafts Movement in both the 19th and 20th centuries. The idea was expressed by William Morris in the middle of the 19th century and repeated constantly thereafter by kindred spirits in Europe and the United States.

Together with the idea that the material and moral fabric of society were connected, there existed an interest in the working conditions under which the artefacts were produced. A building or a piece of furniture true to the aims of the Arts and Crafts tradition had not only to be beautiful but also to be the result of contented labour, in which the craftsman or woman could reject the drudgery and alienation of factory work and delight in simple handicraft. The movement's precursors, Carlyle, and more particularly Ruskin and Morris, had virtually characterized labour as a sacrament. It was through the medium of work, they maintained, that men and women expressed not only their individual creativity but also the essence of their humanity. In his *Lectures on Socialism*, Morris wrote that 'Art is Man's expression of his joy in Labour', an expression that the pressure of industrialized factory work had rendered impossible. Morris continues: 'Since all persons . . . must produce in some form or another it follows that under our present system most honest men must lead unhappy lives since their work . . . is devoid of pleasure'. Or, put more succinctly, that in Victorian society, as far as Morris was concerned, 'happiness is only possible to artists and thieves'.

It was the desire to improve both aesthetic standards and working conditions that generated a further article of faith shared by many active within the Arts and Crafts Movement: the belief that the material and moral fabric of society had been infinitely better some time in the past, be it the England of the Middle Ages or the America of the pioneer age. The ethos of industrial capitalism demanded production for profit rather than need and had generated

shoddily designed goods in the process at the expense of both their aesthetic appeal to consumers and the well-being of the workforce. These miserable conditions were in stark contrast to those of a pre-industrialized past in which, it was generally believed, production took place under far more wholesome conditions. The crafts of medieval society had none of the 'engine-turned precision' of modern industry, but they retained the sense of humanity that Ruskin so admired. Writing on 'The Nature of Gothic' in the second volume of *The Stones of Venice*, published in 1853, Ruskin insisted that: 'You must make either a tool of the creature or a man of him. You cannot make both. Men were not intended to work with the accuracy of tools, to be precise and perfect in all their actions. If you will have that precision out of them, and make their fingers

measure degrees like cog-wheels, and their arms strike curves like compasses, you must unhumanize them.'

Pre-industrial society, then, was understood to retain precisely that element of humanity that industrial capitalism lacked. Men and women were not bound by the relationship of 'master' and 'wage-slave', based on alienating and mechanized factory labour, but lived as a human community centred upon the workshop, where they were employed on useful and creative tasks. The admiration for some romanticized, pre-industrial Utopia was endemic among 19th-century critics of industrialism – so endemic, in fact, that an echo of the sentiment even permeates the *Economic and Philosophical Manuscripts* of Karl Marx (1818–83). Not generally known for his romanticism, Marx found and admired in the working con-

RIGHT
*The Guild Hall,
London, and the Hôtel
de Ville, Paris, from
A.W.N. Pugin's*
Contrasts, *published
in 1836.*

Heaps of garbage and ashes lie in all directions, and the foul liquids emptied before the door gather in stinking pools. Here live the poorest of the poor, the worst paid workers with thieves and the victims of prostitution indiscriminately huddled together, the majority Irish, or of Irish extraction, and those who have not yet sunk in the whirlpool of moral ruin which surrounds them, sinking daily deeper, losing daily more and more of their power to resist the demoralising influence of want, filth, and surroundings.

The sense of loyalty and social responsibility that was understood to have existed between the various levels of society in the previous centuries was now absent. The creed of *laissez-faire* utilitarianism relieved the wealthy from any responsibility toward the poor. Some economists saw the conditions Engels described as an unfortunate but necessary evil. Social life in England was, in the eyes of many critics, gradually being undermined to generate a nation of masters and wage-slaves.

The climate of dissent in the late 18th and 19th centuries took on a variety of forms. At one end of the spectrum was the romantic, celibate 'Brotherhood', dedicated to art and chivalry, conceived by William Morris and Edward Burne-Jones (1833–98) while at Oxford. This fraternity devoted itself to things of the spirit and determined to mask the horrors of industrialism beneath a veneer of art. At the other end of the spectrum Karl Marx and Friedrich Engels saw within industrial society's class-struggle, inevitable revolution and the seeds of its own destruction. At various points between these extremes a host of other critics argued for democratic freedom and the emancipation of the industrial working classes or saw national salvation in the revival of the feudal ideals of a lost past. In many instances there was very little love lost between the factions. These dissenters, whether revolutionary or romantic, were, however, bound by the deep suspicion that was to be shared by artists and artisans of the Arts and Crafts Movement, the suspicion that society under industrialism was getting worse rather than better.

In the first half of the 19th century protests against the horror of the Industrial Revolution were common. The tone of these protests was often ineffectual, serving to create a means of escape from the unpleasantness of Victorian

*BELOW LEFT Interior
view of the Crystal
Palace showing a
display of moving
machinery. The
illustration is taken
from the exhibition
catalogue.*

the exhibition's purpose in her reply to her husband's opening address. She hoped that it would 'conduce to . . . the common interests of the human race by encouraging the arts of peace and industry', and that it would promote 'friendly and honourable rivalry . . . for the good and happiness of mankind'.

Many of Victoria's subjects did not share her appreciation for the fruits of industry and free international trade, and saw the onslaught of industrialization as detrimental to the nation. Since the beginning of the century many commentators had realized that industry had the capacity to generate wealth and misery in equal quantities. William Cobbett, writing as early as 1807, observed that the industrialized city of Coventry maintained a population of 20,000, almost one half of whom were paupers. Industry had generated wealth but concentrated that wealth in the hands of a few people, serving to create 'two nations'. One of the most vivid descriptions of the extent to which wealth had been polarized is given by Friedrich Engels. Writing in *The Condition of the Working Class in England*, he gave a graphic account of the conditions of the urban poor. He stated,

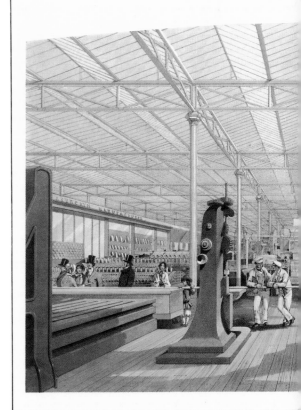

 On 1 May 1851, Britain celebrated its industrial might with the opening of the 'Great Exhibition of all Nations'. The exhibition took place in Joseph Paxton's Crystal Palace, erected in London's Hyde Park. The glass and iron construction, some 1,800 ft (549 m) long, 140 ft (43 m) high and with a volume of 33 million cubic ft (934,000 cubic m), was erected in less than eight months. Sir Matthew Digby, Secretary to the exhibition's Executive Committee, saw this vast undertaking as a reflection of the national character. The size of the venture represented national courage and the nation's strength could be seen in the speed with which it was built. National wealth was displayed in the resources used in the building and the country's intellect symbolized by its architectural complexity. Moreover, the beauty of the Crystal Palace, according to Digby, demonstrated that 'the British are by no means indifferent to the beautiful in fine arts'. The building housed the work of 15,000 exhibitors, which was displayed in four categories: raw materials; machinery; manufactures; sculpture and the fine arts. Queen Victoria summed up

CHAPTER ONE

THE FOUNDING FATHERS

Title page from Clarence Cook's The House Beautiful, *1878.*
The House Beautiful introduced tasteful art and design to an
American bourgeoisie cut off from recent cultural developments in
Europe.

ditions of medieval society – 'an intimate and human side' that was resolutely absent in the factory sweatshops of the industrialized 19th century.

Not all of the ventures that took place under the banner of Arts and Crafts were an unqualified success. William Morris, towards the end of his life, expressed profound doubt about the real value of his work and maintained that the undeniably beautiful work produced by his company was undertaken only for the wealthy. There were, in turn, numerous other well-intentioned craft ventures that began with great optimism only to end in bankruptcy. Morris had stumbled on a paradox that affected all evangelistic craftsmen and women active within the movement in Europe and the United States: objects made by hand are far more expensive than those made by machine and necessarily exclude the disadvantaged masses for whom they were intended. Ultimately, there came to the Arts and Crafts Movement the realization that the social reform demanded by many craftsmen and women could not be achieved by Arts and Crafts alone, and there was a catalogue of attempts to resolve this paradox. In fact, the history of the Arts and Crafts Movement is, in many respects, a history of compromises, and the various solutions to this paradox form the framework of this present study. It begins with the romantic refuge from industrialism sought by the Pre-Raphaelites and their circle in the mid-19th century and goes on to chart the development of the craft fraternities and sororities on both sides of the Atlantic and ends with the establishment of the European and American design factories in this century that compromised earlier romantic ideals and came to terms with mechanized industry.

LEFT American clock in the Gothic style by Brewster and Co., c. 1860. The Gothic style became increasingly important in 19th-century American culture. It is evident in domestic goods and architecture and was seen by some as a less pretentious style than the classical idiom common in the 18th and early 19th centuries.

saw the conditions under which medieval craftsmen worked as infinitely more wholesome than the mechanized drudgery of industrialism, and maintained that it was to the spirit of this medieval model that 19th-century society must turn for salvation. Production, he insisted, would be for use rather than profit and the machine-like precision exchanged for an imperfect human finish. Ruskin explained his ideal of creative work in writing:

Let him but begin to imagine, to think, to try to do anything worth doing; and the engine turned precision is lost at once. Out come all his roughness, all his dullness, all his incapability; shame upon shame, failure upon failure, pause after pause: but out comes the whole majesty of him also.

One of the first architects and designers in Britain to give practical form to an antipathy for the modern industrial environment was Augustus Welby Pugin. Pugin employed an architectural style reminiscent of that of the Middle Ages. He distinguished himself from many other late 18th- and early 19th- century Gothic revivalists by equating the appearance of medieval building with the spiritual refinement of the Middle Ages. The Gothic had long been employed either for its picturesque characteristics or as a nationalistic antidote to the international classical style. Pugin, however, maintained that Gothic was less a style than an architectural representation of Christian sentiment, and was starkly contrasted to the crass and spiritually vacuous utilitarian building of his own age.

In 1835 Pugin wrote *Contrasts: or a Parallel between the Noble Edifices of the Middle Ages, and Corresponding Buildings of the Present Day, shewing the Present Decay of Taste*. The work was an indictment not only of 19th-century taste but also the degenerate industrialized social system from which it emerged. The 'Contrast' between a Catholic town of 1440 and the same town some 400 years later illustrated the sorry state of contemporary building. The 19th-century town showed despoiled medieval churches interspersed among iron and gas works, an asylum and prison. The indictment continued with further contrasts between medieval and modern society: one illustration showed a benign community of well-fed and -clothed poor housed in a medieval monastery, the other the misery of the modern panopti-

RIGHT Grace Church, on New York's Broadway and Tenth Street, by James Renwick, Jr.; completed in 1846.

con. Although Ruskin and Morris dissociated themselves from Pugin (respectively for his Catholicism and his antipathy to working-class movements), the notion that art and architecture carry the capacity to redeem and improve society was an important departure in Gothic revivalist architecture and one that was to recur in many manifestations of the Arts and Crafts Movement both in Europe and in the United States.

Mid-19th-century America began to share the European taste for Gothic architecture. In most cases American builders used the Gothic purely for its picturesque and visual appeal. James Renwick Jr, for example, designer of Grace Church on New York's Lower Broadway and the Smithsonian Institution in Washington, D.C., used the Gothic with little regard for the historical associations the style retained in Britain. Some architects, however, began to adapt and lend their own meaning to the style. The Gothic was seen by some as less pretentious than the sophisticated Greek revival style that had dominated building in the early 19th century. Andrew Jackson Downing (1815–1851), a landscape gardener and writer, saw within the Gothic style an element of honesty and practicality. The style was, he maintained, far better suited to the homespun aspirations of American citizens and could also serve to refine uneducated American tastes, cheapened by the mass-produced *objets d'art* that had flooded markets in the wake of the Industrial Revolution in the United States. Downing's *Cottage Residences,* published in 1842, expressed a strong sense of artistic independence and an affinity with old pioneer values. He wrote:

... every man either builds or looks forward to building a home for himself, at some period of his life; it may be only a log hut or a most rustic cottage, but perhaps also, a villa or a mansion. As yet, however, our houses are mostly either of the plainest and most meagre description, or if of a more ambitious, they are frequently of a more objectionable character – shingle palaces, of very questionable convenience, and not in the least adapted, by their domestic and rural beauty, to harmonise with our lovely natural landscapes.

Downing advocated, in some instances, the use of a more elaborate Gothic style in the design of homes for the wealthy. In general, good domestic American architecture could take its

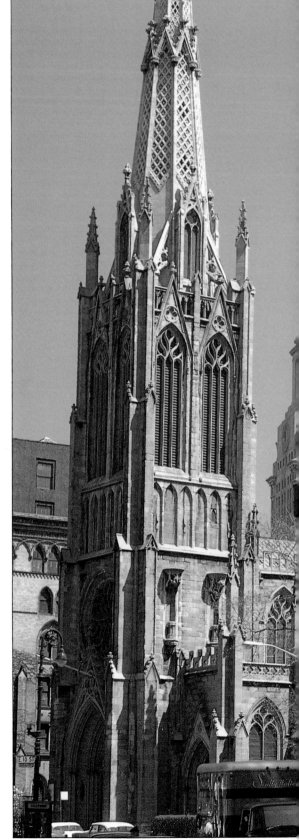

LEFT Design for a
small cottage from
*Andrew Jackson
Downing's* Cottage
Residences, *published
in 1842.*

*BELOW LEFT Detail,
Grace Church, by
James Renwick, Jr.*

[Fig. 87.]

ANDERSON SC.

802

■

*RIGHT Lyndhurst by
Alexander Jackson
Davis; built in
Tarrytown, New York,
in 1838 for William
Paulding.*

lead from the example set by more modest
Tudor Gothic or Tuscan building, simple but
soundly built architecture appropriate to the
independent lifestyle of most rural Americans.

The notion of a specifically American sense
of design and architecture was developed in
the writings of the art collector and critic James
Jackson Jarves (1818–1888). Jarves, a keen collector of late medieval Italian paintings, disliked the way in which European styles were
being inappropriately used for American
building to create 'chaotic, incomplete, and
arbitrary' architecture. Eschewing both 'Bastard
Grecian' and 'Impoverished Gothic', Jarves
advocated a quite independent path that was to
be followed by architects associated with Arts

and Crafts in both Europe and the United
States. Building, Jarves insisted, must be in
harmony with its surroundings. He maintained that architecture grew out of the wants
and ideas of a nation and could not be imported at will from a well of European styles
and influences, be they Greek, Roman or
Gothic. Writing in 1864, Jarves stated:

Our forefathers built simply for protection and
adaptation. Their style of dwelling houses was
suited to the climate, materials at hand, and social
exigencies. Hence it was true and natural. They
could not deal in artifice or plagiarism, because they
had no tricks of beauty to display and nothing to
copy. Over their simple truth of expression time has
thrown the veil of rustic enchantment, so that the

farmhouses still standing of the period of the Indian wars are a much more pleasurable feature of the landscape than their villa-successors of the 19th century.

The development of a sense of artistic independence and the return to the common-sense values of the pioneer primarily occurred in writing rather than shingle, bricks and mortar. There are some exceptions: the architects Alexander Jackson Davis and Richard Upjohn, in particular, stand out. Davis, a friend of Downing, abhorred the symmetry of Greek classicism, preferring the more modest Gothic style: two contrasting examples of his work are the large mansion Lyndhurst, built in Tarrytown, New York, and the less ambitious Rotch House, a comparatively small cottage in New Bedford, Massachusetts. Richard Upjohn – architect of Trinity Church on New York's lower Broadway, believed by some to be the 'greatest church erected in America' – contributed to a more sophisticated understanding of Gothic architecture not dissimilar to that of Pugin. Interpreting church architecture not as a mere style but as a medium for religious devotion, Upjohn, a high churchman, professed to have no interest in the style of a building as an end in itself, but saw the Gothic as an idiom uniquely able to communicate Christian feeling. Architecture was seen as a medium of faith.

LEFT Detail, Lyndhurst.

BELOW LEFT Detail, Lyndhurst.

ABOVE LEFT Shaker chair, 19th century. Shaker furniture anticipated many of the concerns of the Arts and Crafts Movement in the United States.

ABOVE RIGHT Reconstruction of a Shaker interior.

By the middle of the 19th century there was a body of opinion that had begun to question the cultural dominance of Europe, a process that was to continue in one form or another until the Second World War. The antidote to the influence of European taste was a return to homespun values. It is worth noting, however, that these values, which were to provide so fertile an environment for the Arts and Crafts Movement to adapt and evolve in the second half of the century, had existed unchanged in some quarters for well over a century. The Quakers (some of whom later became 'Shaking Quakers' or 'Shakers') who had left England to escape persecution in the 17th and 18th centuries had, as pioneers, established a number of religious and economic communities that anticipated many of the aesthetic and social ideals of the Arts and Crafts Movement. Labour was seen as a sacrament (a sentiment shared by Ruskin, himself connected with the low-church Presbyterians). Some of the socialist ideals in Arts and Crafts workshops had, in turn, echoes in Shaker convictions: wealth was held in common by the community as a whole; work undertaken by men or women was understood to be of equal value, and craft activities took place within a secluded community reminiscent of the craft guilds of the second half of the 19th century. Consistent with an Arts and Crafts aesthetic, Shaker furniture and architecture were simply made, functional and without excessive decoration, and much of it bears a marked resemblance to later ventures by more self-conscious artists and craftsmen. It is interesting to consider that the Industrial Revolution, studiously ignored in the production of much Arts and Crafts furniture, is actually absent in the historical evolution of Shaker crafts. The pre-industrial traditions of the Shakers, imported from 17th-century England, were in many instances the very traditions to which men and women of the Crafts Movement were returning.

We can conclude by saying that the Arts and Crafts Movement in Britain and the United States was built on separate but by no means independent cultural traditions. In Britain, the idea of a pre-industrial, medieval past articulated through the writings of Ruskin, Carlyle and Pugin provided the British Arts and Crafts Movement with a strong sense of the artistic, moral and social refinements of a technologically less sophisticated age. This British ideal of a feudal past has an American counterpart in the image of the pioneer. The traditions on which American arts and crafts developed were those of a respect for work, independence and self-sufficiency, and the desire to fashion a national culture remote from the fanciful notions and historical traditions of Europe. These two separate but linked traditions, which shared a distaste for sophistication, a strong sense of independence and a belief in the sanctity of work, were respectively to determine the shape of Arts and Crafts in Britain and the United States throughout the remainder of the 19th and 20th centuries.

CHAPTER TWO

PRE-RAPHAELITES IN ENGLAND AND THE UNITED STATES

The Girlhood of Mary Virgin *by Dante Gabriel Rossetti, 1848.*

 The Arts and Crafts Movement in Britain emerged, in part, from the works of the Pre-Raphaelite Brotherhood, a group of dissident artists who rejected the conventional artistic opinions of the academic establishment and sought inspiration in the arts, and later in the crafts, of the Middle Ages.

The accepted wisdom in conventional academic circles of the 19th century was that art gradually began to recover from the ignorance of the Dark Ages around the 14th century, steadily to become more refined until it virtually attained perfection during the High Renaissance. For the most part, the ideals of 16th-century painting became enshrined in the Royal Academy, to the extent that those ideas still had enormous influence almost a century after its foundation in 1768. Many of the young painters associated with the Pre-Raphaelite Brotherhood began to reject this academic sophistication in favour of medieval simplicity. Art, they maintained, should be based not upon the refined, philosophical idealism of the Academy but on the less affected and simpler style of painting found in Europe in the 14th and 15th centuries, or in the straightforward appreciation of nature itself. Ford Madox Brown's *Seeds and Fruit of English Poetry,* painted shortly before the formation of the Brotherhood (*c.* 1848), typifies the archaic but still naturalistic style of the Pre-Raphaelites. Brown's picture is divided by Gothic tracery into three sections to resemble a medieval triptych and, following medieval convention, the backgrounds of two of the panels are painted gold. Despite such conventions, the painting is intensely and naturalistically detailed, with great attention afforded to components of relatively minor importance. A suitable medieval and nationalistic subject is also used in preference to the international stock of tired classical subject matter considered suitable for academic painting. In this instance Chaucer reads aloud to Edward the Black Prince, flanked by a pantheon of British poets.

Rejecting the establishment canon that the principles of art were based upon timeless academic ideals embodied in the example of Raphael, the Pre-Raphaelites professed 'to have no master except their own powers of mind and hand, and their own first hand study

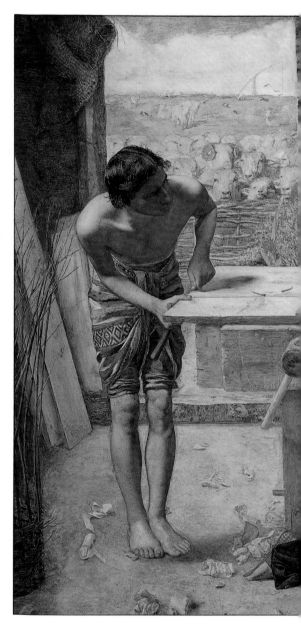

of Nature'. The Brotherhood's secretary, William Michael Rossetti, had succinctly recorded the aims of the movement in an account of the Rossetti family memoirs published in 1895. They were 'to have genuine ideas to express'; 'to study nature attentively'; and 'to sympathise with what is direct and heartfelt in previous art, to the exclusion of what is conventional and self parading and learned by rote'.

The Pre-Raphaelite Brotherhood was founded in London. Initially called 'Early Christian', the movement abandoned the name for fear of Roman Catholic associations. The

Brotherhood consisted of seven members: Dante Gabriel and William Michael Rossetti, John Everett Millais, William Holman Hunt, F.G. Stephens and Thomas Woolner, together with a handful of fellow-travellers, among them Burne-Jones and Morris.

One of the first pictures to bear the enigmatic stamp PRB (Pre-Raphaelite Brotherhood) was Dante Gabriel Rossetti's 'symbol of female excellence', *The Girlhood of Mary Virgin*, painted in 1848. Following the advice given by Ruskin, the broad and generalized impression of nature found in academic painting was rejected and every item in the picture depicted in

minute detail. A contemporary account of Rossetti at work recorded him painting in oils with fine watercolour brushes on a perfectly smooth white surface to achieve the detailed and translucent effect gained by 'primitive' artists of 15th-century Italy. Again, the choice of subject was unconventional. The picture shows an adolescent Mary surrounded by symbols that pre-figure her role as 'Mary, pre-elect God's Virgin'. A sonnet accompanying the picture when it was first exhibited at the Free Exhibition of 1849 explained the intense symbolism within the picture: the red cloth in the background – a symbol of Christ's passion –

RIGHT A Converted
British Family
Sheltering a
Christian Missionary
from the
Persecution of the
Druids *by William
Holman Hunt, 1850.*

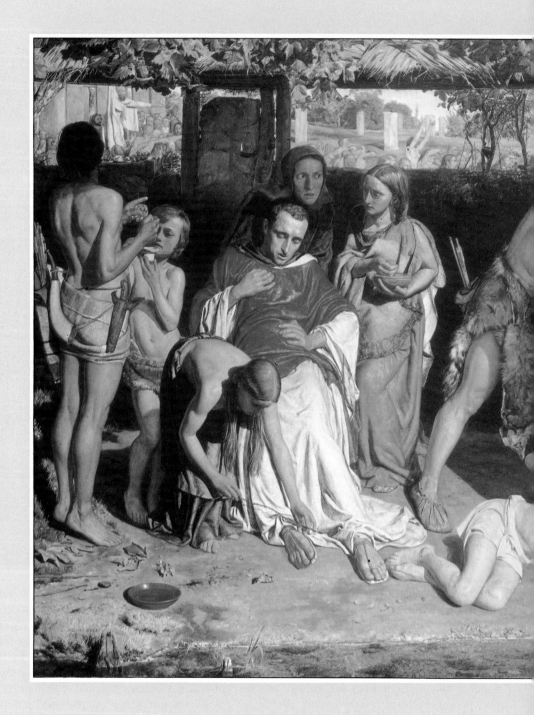

carries a tri-point, 'perfect each except the second of its points, to teach that Christ is not yet born'; the books represent the Virtues; the lamp – Piety; the lily symbolizes innocence and the vine pre-figures Christ's coming.

Other paintings in a similarly archaic, but invariably naturalistic style followed. John Everett Millais' *Isabella*, the first of his pictures to bear the insignia PRB, was taken from Keats' reworking of Boccaccio's account of the love affair between Lorenzo and Isabella from the *Decameron*. Millais painted the work in intricate detail and, in keeping with demands for historical accuracy, took the costume designs from recently published historical accounts of medieval Italian dress. Equally detailed is Millais' *Christ in the House of his Parents,* painted in 1849 and exhibited the following year at the Royal Academy. Pre-figurative symbols abound: among them nails, stigmata, baptismal bowls, sheep, doves and so on. Similar components are found within William Holman Hunt's *A Converted British Family Sheltering a Christian Missionary from the Persecution of the Druids* of 1850. The sheltered missionary serves as the figure of Christ, and the boy with the bowl to the left as John the Baptist; the water and bowl in the foreground again symbolize baptism, and the thorn and sponge held by the two young girls symbolize the Passion. The turn of mind of many Pre-Raphaelite painters of the period was such that in the search for a more meaningful 'heartfelt' style of painting to up-stage conventional academicism, the absence of symbolism became more remarkable than its presence – an arcane literary or religious backdrop was an invariable component of British Pre-Raphaelite painting.

Many of the characteristics of Pre-Raphaelite painting, its admiration for the sentiments of a medieval past, its tendency toward simplicity and its emphasis on individual, personal expression rather than established convention, began to find their way into crafts. The main catalyst in this process was the catholic interests of William Morris.

Morris came into contact with the Pre-Raphaelites in 1856, having read of the movement in *The Germ*, the Brotherhood's short-lived magazine, while at Oxford. Heavily under Rossetti's influence, and convinced that painting was the only proper medium to express one's disapproval of industrialism,

RIGHT Attic bedroom of William Morris's Kelmscott Manor, containing examples of green-stained furniture designed by Ford Madox Brown, c. 1861. In an attempt to unite the fine and applied arts, a number of Pre-Raphaelites tried their hand at a variety of crafts with varying degrees of success.

BELOW RIGHT Gothic sideboard designed by Philip Webb, c. 1862. Ebonized wood with painted and leather panels.

Morris and Burne-Jones set up a studio in Red Lion Square in London. Morris's abilities as a painter were somewhat limited (as his only extant oil painting, that of *Queen Guenevere*, indicates), and his interest in the medium was temporary. It was, however, around this period that Morris began designing some items of 'intensely medieval' furniture for the studio at Red Lion Square, and Pre-Raphaelite interest in art began to stray into other media. Several chairs and a table were made, together with an oak settle so large that Burne-Jones complained that it took up one-third of the studio. Rossetti decorated the panels on the settle with scenes depicting *Love between the Sun and the Moon* and *The Meeting of Dante and Beatrice in Florence*. More ambitious collaborative schemes soon followed when Morris moved from Red Lion Square into the Red House, near Bexleyheath in Kent.

LEFT Queen
Guenevere *by
William Morris, 1858.*

THE RED HOUSE

The Red House, one of the first examples of Arts and Crafts architecture, was completed for Morris and his new wife Jane Burden in 1860 by Philip Webb, a student of the architect George Edmond Street, to whom Morris had also once been articled. It was originally intended that the Red House be the home of a romantic community of artists and craftsmen, although the idea seems not to have been taken seriously by anyone other than Morris. The style of the house is very simple. The exterior is of the local plain red brick and is capped by a steeply pitched tile roof reminiscent of domestic Tudor buildings. The interior of the house is equally restrained. Consistent with the utilitarian Arts and Crafts aesthetic that no undue effort should be made to disguise materials or structure, the staircase was originally left unpanelled to render its structure visible, and the construction of the roof can be clearly seen from the rooms on the first floor. The general simplicity of the white-washed interior was offset by opulent pieces of furniture, painted glass, embroidery and fresco painting, collaboratively designed by one or more

of the artists and craftsmen associated with the Pre-Raphaelites. The furniture of the period echoed many of the features found in contemporary Pre-Raphaelite painting. Contemporary taste for refined machine-finished furniture was rejected and craftsmen used a heavy, rugged style reminiscent of the then unfashionable Tudor or Caroline periods. In some instances, such as the settle designed by Webb for the hall at the Red House, the furniture was very simple. In other examples, the furniture was decorated with minutely detailed painting. Other contributions to the house included

LEFT The Red House, designed by Philip Webb and built in 1859 for William Morris at Bexleyheath, Kent.

a variety of *métiers*, from furniture-making to fresco painting. The Pre-Raphaelite *oeuvre* and its 'Palace of Art' at the Red House had, as yet, only served to create a secluded community and a means of escape from Victorian social ills. Protected by Morris's independent income from mines in Cornwall, the painters and craftsmen and women active at the Red House were able to ignore the political revolutions throughout Europe. Like many romantics, Morris and Rossetti had expressed an aristocratic disdain for politics and current worldly events. Instead, their attention was focused on the design of an imaginary medieval world of chivalrous rather than practical values. The revolutionary spirit and desire for social change on which subsequent Arts and Crafts ventures were predicated had yet to appear in the works of Morris and his contemporaries. The desire to challenge rather than avoid the horrors of industrialism was, however, beginning to emerge and was among the ideals of the 'Fine Art Workmen' active in Morris, Marshall, Faulkner and Co.

Burne-Jones' painted glass designs in the long gallery and wall paintings in the drawing room. The ceiling contained decorations by Jane and William Morris and the former had embroidered hangings for the walls. Rossetti painted scenes from Dante's *Divine Comedy* on some items of furniture and contributed fragments to the painted ceiling.

The work produced by Morris and his associates, although original and very impressive, was, at this stage, still very romantic. The Pre-Raphaelites had tilted at Victorian convention, and their distaste for prevailing aesthetic standards found expression in

∎

RIGHT Apple
Blossoms *by John
William Hill.*

While the first ventures in Arts and Crafts were being undertaken at the Red House, another community of painters inspired by Ruskin's example was forming in the United States, a society called the Association for the Advancement of Truth in Art. The Association, often overlooked in accounts of Pre-Raphaelite painting, is interesting as it anticipates the direction of the Arts and Crafts Movement in the United States, a direction based not upon the medievalism of the British Arts and Crafts Movement, but rather on the search for an independent aesthetic conducive to American geography, culture and ideology. *The New Path,* the Association's journal, clarified some of these intentions in its first issue of 1861. Its opening statement read:

The future of art in America is not without hope . . . . The artists are nearly all young men; they are not hampered by too many traditions, and they enjoy almost inestimable advantage of having no past, no masters and no schools. Add that they work for an unsophisticated and, as far as art is concerned, uneducated public, which whatever else may stand in the way, will not be prevented by any prejudice or pre-conceived notions from accepting any really good work which may be set before it!

The Association had been founded on Ruskinian principles and modelled itself on the British Brotherhood. Although medieval subject matter did not really appeal to artists 'with no past', the notion that Nature rather than old academic tradition (and in this instance old European academic tradition) should serve as the prime source of inspiration

in art had a strong appeal for artists searching for a cultural identity of their own.

The Association was established through a series of meetings around 1863, along lines similar to its British counterpart. Many of the painters and critics who were connected with the Association had long been aware of the Pre-Raphaelites through a magazine entitled *The Crayon,* published between 1855 and 1863. The magazine carried articles on Pre-Raphaelite painting and contained extracts of articles by Ruskin, already known in the United States for two enthusiastically received works, *Modern Painters* and *Elements of Drawing.*

The Association was established under the direction of Charles Farrer, a painter educated, in part, by Ruskin and Rossetti at the Working Men's College in London. It was Farrer who established a committee and the Association's articles. In essence, the Association was to be a fraternity dedicated to educating American artists and their public. Like its British counterpart, members of the Association were often declamatory and stridently anti-establishment. Its professed aim was to generate an air of dissatisfaction with the American art establishment and the academic theories to which it subscribed. Academic painters and sculptors were frequently subjected to savage criticism in *The New Path.* For example, the works of Thomas Cole, a painter of genteel landscapes in the English picturesque tradition and a pillar of the academic establishment, were dubbed as not being worth the canvas they were painted on. Cole was violently censured for his dependence on an out-

moded and alien tradition. Contrasted against the works of Cole and his peers were the intensely naturalistic pictures of Henry Hills, Charles Moore, Jonathan Sturgis, Farrer and a group of artists and critics that by the end of 1863 was to number well over 20. Hills' 1863 study, *Buttermilk Falls*, consistent with Ruskin's demands, selects and rejects nothing. Whereas more conventional American painters, like their European counterparts, sought to give general impressions of a landscape, Hills painted in such detail that it was possible to identify the geology of a landscape through the factual detail in the painted rock. No one particular part of Hills' pictures ever assumes importance. Painters connected with the Association invariably worked in an almost mechanical fashion, thereby giving each component the most minute attention.

Farrer's *Gone Gone* epitomizes an equally naturalistic but more anecdotal facet of American Pre-Raphaelite-inspired painting. The picture was painted in 1860 but appears originally to have escaped the notice of the press. It was brought to public attention several years later by the critic Clarence Cook, a staunch supporter of the Association and its work. Unlike its British equivalents, such as Millais' *A Huguenot on the Eve of St. Bartholomew's Day* – a print of which appears in the corner of Farrer's painting – *Gone Gone* is not extracted directly from a known literary source or historical event. The painting only alludes to some loss or tragic parting. Symbolism, again, abounds, with images of loss or death such as autumn leaves, the setting sun, and an extract from the Gospel according to St Matthew.

The Association lost much of its impetus by the late 1860s, although individual painters continued to work along similar lines. Clarence Cook, who had hitherto supported the Association, stated that he considered the achievements of Farrer and his contemporaries to be limited and that their painting, although superficially impressive, lacked real depth. By this time *The New Path* had ceased publication and artists connected with the Association failed to show works at the American Watercolor Society, a venue it had helped to establish. It eventually disbanded and Farrer and Moore left for Europe.

The achievements of the Association for the Advancement of Truth in Art were limited. Unlike the Pre-Raphaelite movement in Britain, it did not act as a springboard for a wealth of further developments in the arts and crafts. However, the advent of an American response to Ruskin's theories lends weight to the existence of a gradually evolving nationalistic artistic consciousness on which subsequent Arts and Crafts ventures were nurtured.

BELOW LEFT Wall cabinet designed by Philip Webb, c. 1861–62, and painted with scenes from the life of St George by William Morris.

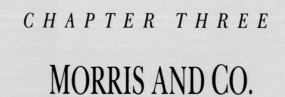

CHAPTER THREE

MORRIS AND CO.

Christ Suffering the Little Children, *designed by Edward
Burne-Jones in 1862 in collaboration with the firm of Morris,
Marshall, Faulkner and Co., for the Church of All Saints, Selsley,
Gloucestershire.*

The firm of Morris, Marshall, Faulkner and Co. was established in April 1861. The company was of unparalleled importance in the Arts and Crafts Movement and established theoretical and practical precedents that were followed by similar communities in Europe and the United States. The beginnings of Morris, Marshall, Faulkner and Co., however, were rather uncertain. Rossetti, one of the founder members of the firm, recounted some years later that the idea of this business venture began as little more than a joke. A discussion began among some of the painters and architects who had designed and decorated the Red House regarding the way in which artists of the Middle Ages undertook not only painting and sculpture but also many other *métiers*. A small sum of money was raised as capital and Rossetti, Madox Brown, Burne-Jones, Webb, P.P. Marshall, C.J. Faulkner and Morris decided to establish their own community of 'fine art workmen'. Faulkner was to be the firm's bookkeeper and Morris, the only member with sufficient time and money to devote himself entirely to the company, was elected manager. The firm's prospectus declared its intentions. Diversely working in stained glass, mural decoration, carving, metalwork, furniture and embroidery, Morris, Marshall, Faulkner and Company lent its weight to the reform of the decorative arts in England.

Morris was later to explain the importance of the decorative or 'Lesser Arts' in a lecture given to the Trades Guild of Learning in 1877. He maintained that it was only comparatively recently that these 'lesser' decorative arts had become divorced from the fine arts of painting and sculpture. The division between these two forms of creative labour had, he maintained, served to trivialize the decorative arts and reduce the finer arts of painting and sculpture to a 'dull adjunct to unmeaning pomp'. The decorative arts, properly reconstituted according to old medieval traditions, had a noble calling. They were, for Morris, akin to a democratic, popular art. 'Our subject', he wrote, 'is that great body of art, by means of which men have at all times striven to beautify the familiar matters of everyday life'.

Morris described decorative art historically as a natural form of human feeling and expression, as an 'art of the unconscious intelli-

LEFT A Scene from the Annunciation *by Edward Burne-Jones, 1860, for St Columba's Church, Topcliffe, Yorkshire.*

gence'. 'Everything', he wrote, 'made by man's hand has a form which must be either beautiful or ugly'. If the craftsman or woman follows the example of Nature on his or her design, the result, Morris maintained, will necessarily be beautiful. If Nature's example is ignored, the product will turn out to be ugly. Morris neatly described beautiful decoration as an 'alliance with nature'. The craftsman or woman must work in the way that Nature does 'till the web, the cup or the knife, look as natural, nay as lovely, as the green field, the river bank, or the mountain flint'.

The decorative arts had a formidable opponent in the philistinism of the Victorian middle classes. Since the Great Exhibition of 1851, which, incidently, the young Morris refused to visit, English taste had been dominated by an eclectic style not dissimilar to the bourgeois taste prevalent in the United States. The furniture of the period was absurdly decorative, with gilt, veneers, and marble used at every opportunity. Moreover, such goods were invariably machine-made and often of very poor quality. For Morris, the source of this 'design debauchery' (as Walter Crane was later to describe Victorian taste) was twofold. Firstly, ill-educated and penny-pinching consumers were anxious to get sumptuous furniture at the lowest possible price. This in turn provided a ready market that avaricious manufacturers were only too eager to supply. Using the ingenuity of machine production and the aesthetics of the counting-house, Britain therefore turned out a constant supply of goods of dubious quality and even more dubious taste. The mission of the handicraftsman was a formidable one: to educate and reform public taste and also to reform the means of production and consumption. This socialist aesthetic is neatly summarized in *The Lesser Arts*, in which Morris wrote:

To give people pleasure in the things they must perforce *use*, that is one great office of decoration; to give people pleasure in the things they must perforce *make*, that is the other use of it.

Several of the design projects of Morris, Marshall, Faulkner and Co. well illustrated this statement, especially the joint endeavours involving their own domiciles that were undertaken by the firm's principals and assorted friends and relatives.

The firm's first commissions came, predominantly, from the church, and were the result of the High Anglican interest in church ritual and decoration that, in part, had stimulated an interest in Gothic revivalist architecture. Also, the foundation of the firm had initially prompted fierce opposition from other manufacturers, to the extent that ecclesiastical commissions were one of the few segments of the market to which the company had easy access. Among the earlier commissions were those of the architect G.F. Bodley. Bodley had used some examples of stained glass designed by Madox Brown, Burne-Jones and Rossetti for his newly built churches of St Michael's, Brighton, E. Sussex; All Saints, Selsley, Gloucestershire; St Martin's on the Hill, Scarborough, Yorkshire, and All Saints in Cambridge. Messrs Morris and Co. had also decorated other parts of the interior of St Martin's, contributing a painted mural and two painted panels on the pulpit. Other ecclesiastical commissions followed, among them Madox Brown's work for St Oswald's Church, Durham, and one of the few examples of stained glass by Morris himself – a figure of St Paul, for the Church of St Giles in Camberwell, London.

FAR LEFT Stained-glass window depicting Miriam, the sister of Moses and Aaron, by Edward Burne-Jones, 1872.

CENTRE LEFT Part of a scene depicting the Flight into Egypt, designed by Edward Burne-Jones in collaboration with Morris and Co., for St Michael's Church in Brighton.

LEFT Detail of Flight into Egypt by Edward Burne-Jones, St Michael's Church, Brighton.

FAR LEFT, BELOW Stained-glass window showing King David, from a design by William Morris.

BELOW Scenes from the Life of Christ by Burne-Jones and Morris, 1864.

One of the company's first secular commissions was the decoration of a massive cabinet to the design of the architect J. P. Seddon. Madox Brown, Rossetti and Burne-Jones collaborated on the decoration for the cabinet: an allegory of the arts in the form of a series of scenes from the honeymoon of King René of Anjou. Around this period Philip Webb designed several pieces of similarly elaborate furniture. Characteristic of the firm's early style was the ebonized and painted sideboard with illuminated panels that had been included in the company's catalogue of 1862. Experiments in other media followed. A series of designs for wallpapers was produced and printed. Morris initially attempted to expand the technique of printing and master the craft himself, although difficulties occurred and the work was sent to an independent contractor. In 1864 Webb had helped to design some of the wallpapers.

'Trellis', an early design inspired by the garden at the Red House, contains a climbing rose, a trellis and a bird by Webb. Morris's wallpaper design 'Daisy', produced in the same year, was inspired by a French illuminated manuscript and was also used both as a design for a piece of embroidery and ceramic tiles. Several other artists and designers had contributed some ceramic designs on plain tiles imported from the Netherlands, among them Rossetti, Burne-Jones, Brown, Kate and Lucy Faulkner and, not least, William De Morgan. Jane Morris and her sister Elizabeth Burden had also supervised the production of embroidered cloth and silk, one of the few skills undertaken by women employees.

The fortunes of the company were at first precarious. J.W. Mackail, Morris's biographer, mentioned that the firm failed to make any substantial profits during its first years. Its fortunes changed, however, after the International Exhibition of 1862, to which the company contributed specimens of glass, ironwork, embroidery and furniture. Important secular commissions to decorate the Dining Room at the South Kensington Museum (now the Victoria and Albert Museum) and the Tapestry and Armoury Room at St James's Palace followed the exhibition, after which the firm seems to have prospered.

The majority of the company's earlier work was expensive. The South Kensington

RIGHT Oak cabinet designed by J. P. Seddon and decorated with scenes from the honeymoon of King René of Anjou by Madox Brown, Burne-Jones, Morris and Rossetti, 1862.

BELOW RIGHT The William Morris Room in the Victoria and Albert Museum, London. The windows are by Burne-Jones; the screen by Jane and William Morris; the piano's gesso work by Kate Faulkner, and the walls by Philip Webb.

Museum had complained about the cost of the Green Dining Room and other observers had noted that 'it required a long purse to live up to the higher phases of Morrisean taste'. In addition to the opulently decorated settles and wardrobes produced by Webb and Burne-Jones, there were attempts to produce for those of more modest means. Madox Brown produced some items of simply made 'artisan' furniture, objects of straightforward utility with virtually no decoration whatsoever. Some of these items were, in fact, produced before the foundation of the firm. However, the most famous example of the simpler form of furniture produced by Morris and Co. was the 'Sussex' range of chairs. This 'Good Citizen's' furniture, as it was also known, was based on vernacular designs of country furniture that dated back to the 18th century. The Sussex range was very much cheaper than many of the company's other products, costing from seven to thirty-five shillings, and was certainly within the pockets of the middle classes. It is interesting to observe, however, that the Sussex range, contrary to the ethos of the Arts and Crafts Movement, was produced using some very sophisticated techniques: the wood used for the furniture, for instance, was ebonized, a technique used in 19th-century furniture production to disguise cheap materials.

In 1874 Morris began some of his first experiments in dyeing silk and woollen yarns for embroidery. In keeping with the best Arts and Crafts traditions, the dyestuffs came from natural sources such as indigo, cochineal and madder, the latter a dye with unusual chemical properties rendering it difficult to use with consistency and precision. The first of the famous 'Marigold' designs, printed in madder by Thomas Wardle, followed in 1875. Under Wardle's supervision, Morris tried his hand at the craft during the following year, having researched traditional dyeing methods from old French and English technical manuals. It was around this period that Morris also began to

experiment with woven textiles and carpets. A French weaver helped set up a Jacquard loom and Morris began research into the tapestry collection at the South Kensington Museum. His designs were often taken from early Renaissance needlework, with Morris expressing a characteristic dislike of the more sophisticated patterns and techniques of the 17th and 18th centuries.

In 1874 the firm was reorganized under Morris's sole direction. In recent years the company had prospered and began to influence the work of its competitors. Showrooms for its products were opened in 1877 in Oxford Street and the company had also expanded its interests to incorporate commercial weaving, dyeing and printing with its other activities. In 1881 attempts were made to find more spacious premises to accommodate all of the firm's work under one roof. Morris had initially favoured the conversion of a picturesque disused mill near his country home Kelmscott Manor, Oxfordshire, although its distance from London made it economically less viable than the premises at Merton Abbey, Surrey, only seven miles from the centre of the capital.

CHAPTER THREE

■

LEFT Chair produced by Morris and Co. in ebonized wood with original woollen tapestry with bird motif. Chairs of this design were widely copied both in England and the United States.

Production began at Merton Abbey at the end of 1881 and marked the beginning of one of the firm's most prolific periods. A variety of chintz patterns was produced with the use of old printing techniques. In addition, a series of tapestries was made at the Abbey. Morris had especially trained three young assistants, finding that small fingers were better suited to the craft, and purposely selected average rather than gifted recruits on the Ruskinian premise that creative ability was latent in any intelligent worker. A variety of artists and designers collaborated on the tapestries: the painter and illustrator Walter Crane designed 'Goose Girl' in 1883; Morris, with the assistance of Webb, designed the 'Woodpecker' and 'Forest' tapestries, and Burne-Jones was instrumental in the design of a series on the subject of the Holy Grail for Webb's Standen Hall, in W. Sussex. William De Morgan worked, albeit temporarily, at Merton Abbey producing ceramic tiles, and stained-glass designs were undertaken with the proviso that the firm would only accept contracts working for newly built churches. Morris had recently been in-strumental in founding the Society for the Pro-

tection of Ancient Buildings, an organization that had successfully prevented the restoration or demolition of a number of famous buildings, from Canterbury Cathedral to San Marco in Venice. The Society demanded that the restoration of ancient monuments be undertaken with the minimum of alteration to the existing fabric. Morris's firm, consequently, declined any offer to contribute modern additions to old buildings; the last recorded stained-glass contract for anything other than a comparatively recent example of church architecture, according to Philip Henderson's monograph on Morris, was Burne-Jones' work at Salisbury Cathedral in 1878.

The working conditions at Merton Abbey described by a number of contemporary observers were nothing short of idyllic. The accommodation was light and spacious and set in the countryside beside the river Wandle. Like the craftsmen and women of the Middle Ages, Morris's workers were, according to one observer, free to interpret and add their own personality to many of the designs. Men were involved in the production of most crafts save carpets, which were hand-made by women at

LEFT 'Michaelmas Daisy' wallpaper designed by Morris and Co., first produced in 1912.

Both illustrations show an armchair from the 'Sussex' range by Morris and Co.

the cost to the customer of no less than four guineas per square yard. Morris's workers apparently went unhurriedly about their respective crafts, striving, unlike similar industries in Victorian society, for standards of excellence and beauty rather than quantity.

By the end of the 1880s, Morris and Co. had become something of a nursery for the Arts and Crafts Movement, with many of its artists and craftsmen going on to work independently or to form guilds or associations inspired by Morris's aesthetic and social ideals. Walter Crane, for example, carried out designs for Morris and in 1883 joined the Socialist League and was instrumental in the founding of the Art Workers' Guild. Also active in the Guild was W.A.S. Benson, a designer, metalworker and director of Morris and Co. George Jack, the American-born architect and designer responsible for some of the more sophisticated mahogany furniture produced by the firm in the 1880s, later succeeded Webb in his archi-

LEFT The Orchard, *left-hand fragment of high-warp tapestry by William Morris and J.H. Dearle, c. 1890.*

BELOW LEFT Painting of the pond at Merton Abbey, Surrey, by Lexdon Lewis Pocock (1850–1919). Morris signed the lease for the converted print works 7 June 1881, and thereafter it was a centre for much of his company's work.

tectural practice. Arthur Heygate Mack-murdo's Century Guild, established in 1882, was inspired by the examples of Morris and Ruskin, as was the architect and designer Ernest Gimson. However, the 1880s, the period during which the firm was commercially most successful, also marks an important shift in Morris's opinion on the value of the Arts and Crafts. His interest in the Utopian ideals of the ever-expanding ranks of artists and craftsmen had begun to vacillate. When, for example, T.J. Cobden-Sanderson, a disaffected lawyer eager to work with his hands, entertained the idea of taking up bookbinding at Jane Morris's suggestion, the surprised lawyer found Morris scathing about the purpose of some Utopian guilds of printers dedicated to the production of beautiful books.

The firm had originally been established as an antidote to and buttress against the shoddy philistinism of the upper and middle classes, yet, decades after its foundation, little had visibly changed in Victorian society. Morris and Co. may have been commercially successful, yet the 'holy crusade' waged against the age was far from won. Industrial society continued to produce shoddy goods and had perversely warmed to, and imitated, Morris's work, often with the aid of machinery. His patrons, moreover, ironically came from that section of society that had some responsibility for perpetuating the social conditions he so hated, for good design made under humane and fulfilling working conditions was – as critics had already noted – nothing if not expensive. Morris eventually realized that the capacity of the arts alone to challenge industrial society was severely limited, and so his attitude to the other ventures in the arts and crafts that imitated his example (among them Cobden-Sanderson's 'Dove Press') became, at times, less than enthusiastic. Morris, it appears, still strongly upheld the principles that formed the bedrock of the Arts and Crafts Movement. Beautiful, often simple, handmade objects were invariably preferable to anything that profit-mongering, industrial capitalism could offer, yet Morris continued to nurse the nagging doubt that art on its own was merely a palliative. Writing to Georgiana Burne-Jones in 1882, Morris described the bulk of his efforts as nothing but make-believe. Action was therefore required in a sphere outside the

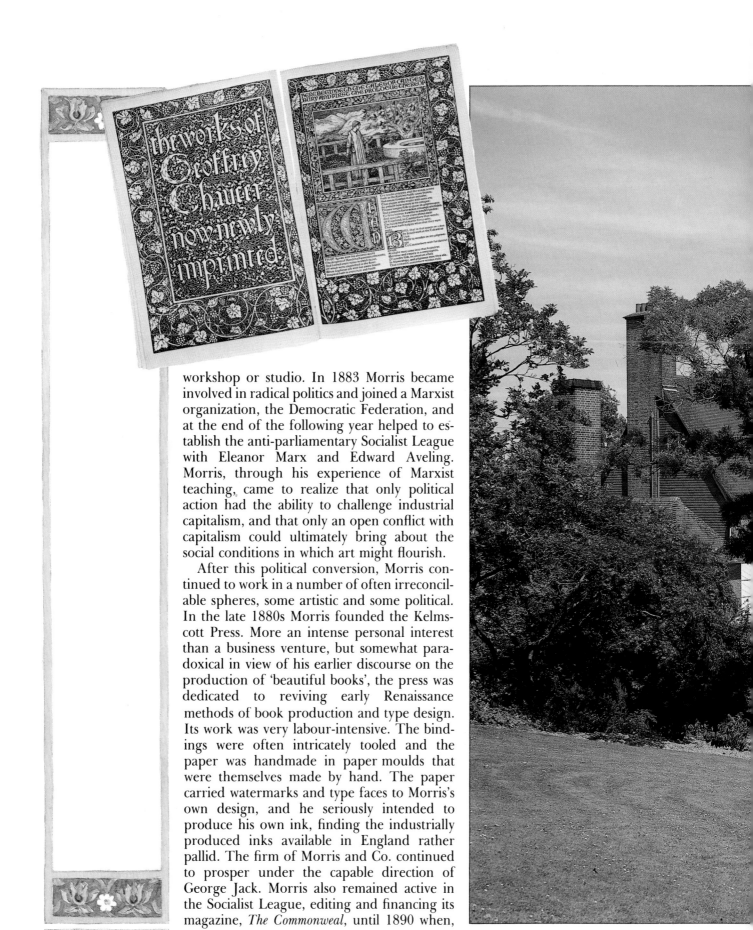

workshop or studio. In 1883 Morris became involved in radical politics and joined a Marxist organization, the Democratic Federation, and at the end of the following year helped to establish the anti-parliamentary Socialist League with Eleanor Marx and Edward Aveling. Morris, through his experience of Marxist teaching, came to realize that only political action had the ability to challenge industrial capitalism, and that only an open conflict with capitalism could ultimately bring about the social conditions in which art might flourish.

After this political conversion, Morris continued to work in a number of often irreconcilable spheres, some artistic and some political. In the late 1880s Morris founded the Kelmscott Press. More an intense personal interest than a business venture, but somewhat paradoxical in view of his earlier discourse on the production of 'beautiful books', the press was dedicated to reviving early Renaissance methods of book production and type design. Its work was very labour-intensive. The bindings were often intricately tooled and the paper was handmade in paper moulds that were themselves made by hand. The paper carried watermarks and type faces to Morris's own design, and he seriously intended to produce his own ink, finding the industrially produced inks available in England rather pallid. The firm of Morris and Co. continued to prosper under the capable direction of George Jack. Morris also remained active in the Socialist League, editing and financing its magazine, *The Commonweal*, until 1890 when,

∎

FAR LEFT The title page and first page of The Works of Geoffrey Chaucer, *printed by Morris's Kelmscott Press in 1896. Known as* The Kelmscott Chaucer, *the book was hand-printed in red and black and bound in pigskin.*

LEFT Standen, near East Grinstead, Sussex. Designed by Philip Webb in 1892 for James Beale, a London solicitor. The house contains works by Morris, W.A.S. Benson and George Jack, together with a number of other employees of Morris and Co.

RIGHT Frontispiece from William Morris's Utopian novel, News from Nowhere, *showing the east front of Kelmscott Manor in Oxfordshire, where the final chapter of this book is set.*

after a schism with an anarchist faction, he established the Hammersmith Socialist Society. He also continued to write poetry and prose. During this period he wrote *News from Nowhere*, the novel that elaborated precisely the revolutionary society to which Morris had aspired in his art and politics.

Morris died in 1896, having made a vast contribution to the practical and intellectual development of the principles of the Arts and Crafts Movement. In fact, so substantial was Morris's contribution, that his progression from the romanticism of the 1860s to his revolutionary opinions of the late 1880s and 1890s pointed to many of the contradictions that subsequent artists and craftsmen were to face in the 19th and 20th centuries. Long after Morris, many craftsmen and women continued to nurse the romantic hope that art still had the ability to challenge the *bête noire* of capitalist industry. Morris, however, had clearly demonstrated that the conditions necessary to create a wholesome and popular art, craft and architecture demanded the overthrow of industrial society. It is no accident that in *News from Nowhere* the Utopian simplicity to which he had aspired was achieved only after a violent revolution.

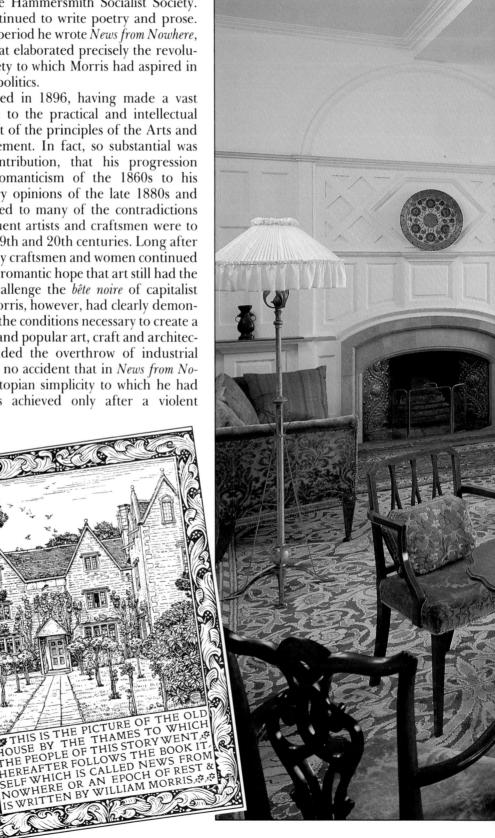

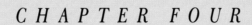

CHAPTER FOUR

THE CRAFT GUILD IN BRITAIN

Design by William Burges for St Mary's, Aldford-cum-Studley,
Yorkshire, c. 1872. Watercolour by Axel Naig.

RIGHT Earthenware painted dish with peacock motif by William De Morgan.

In the decades following the foundation of Morris and Co., a number of craft guilds were created in Britain, the majority by young architects from established practices, eager to revive craft traditions and to reconcile architecture with the decorative arts. They all insisted upon the dignity of work, and those such as Crane and Ashbee mobilized socialism to render labour as a predicate upon which not only healthy and beautiful art was based but also a healthier and more wholesome society. As before, all those involved insisted upon the dignity of work. Ruskin was among the first to try his hand at one such Utopian guild community. However, his Utopia was based not so much upon socialism but upon the romanticized feudalism discussed above. Despite his importance to the Arts and Crafts Movement, Ruskin's efforts to challenge in the form of the paternalistic Guild of St George were by far the most impractical and unsuccessful of the cluster of communities that developed in the wake of Morris and Co.

The foundation of Ruskin's Guild was announced in the eighth of a series of letters written 'to the Workmen and Labourers of Great Britain', the *Fors Clavigera* of May and August 1871. The community was to appeal to 'all holy and humble men of heart' sufficiently

disillusioned with the state of society to help establish an alternative. The alternative proposed by Ruskin was very far removed from the socialism of Morris. The Guild was to be an authoritarian community with Ruskin as its master, below whom came the Guild's three social orders: the *comites ministrantes*, companion servants or administrators; *comites militantes*, or labourers, and finally *comites consilii*, friends active in the world outside, making donations of one-tenth of their income to the Guild. In theory, however, the Guild was to sustain itself by working the land, notably without the aid of steam machinery. The eight clauses of the Guild's charter demanded, first, a love of God. The love of any god was sufficient: the community accommodated all faiths and excluded only atheists. Other demands included a love of one's country and one's fellow man; a respect for labour, beauty and beasts. Ruskin also made a list of appropriate reading material to be included in all of the Guild's homes and aimed to establish a museum. The achievements of the Guild, despite Ruskin's persistent efforts, were modest. He had initially hoped that his pseudo-feudal communities would spread throughout England and beyond. In fact, they were established only near Sheffield, in Barmouth in Wales, and on the Isle of Man.

CHAPTER FOUR
■

*LEFT A series of
underglazed
earthenware tiles by
William De Morgan.*

THE CENTURY GUILD

Inspired by the example of Ruskin, Arthur Heygate Mackmurdo's Century Guild was infinitely more successful than that of his mentor. A pupil in Ruskin's Oxford drawing class and a companion on his visits to Italy, Mackmurdo established the Guild on the advice of his teacher in 1882. In the following year the Century Guild's workshops were opened in partnership with another of Ruskin's associates, Selwyn Image. Image, a former curate, worked in several media, including graphic design (he designed the title page for the Century Guild's magazine, *The Hobby Horse*), embroidery and stained glass. Other members of the Guild included the potter William De Morgan, the designer Heywood Sumner, the sculptor Benjamin Creswick, the textile designer and metalworker H.P. Horne, and the metalworker Clement Heaton. Mackmurdo had trained as an architect but had, in addition, attempted to learn several crafts himself, trying his hand at brasswork, embroidery and cabinetmaking. The purpose of the Century Guild was to accommodate craftsmen active in a number of *métiers* and unite the traditionally separate disciplines of architecture, interior design and decoration.

Whereas Morris had attempted to level the disciplines of painting and sculpture to the rank of democratic handicrafts, Mackmurdo's Century Guild aimed to raise the status of crafts such as building, fabric design, pottery, and metalworking in order that they might take their place alongside the professionally respectable 'fine' arts.

The work of Mackmurdo and the Century Guild tended to be more stylistically eclectic than that of Morris and Co., although it aspired to the same ideal of artists, architects and designers cooperatively undertaking the design of a home and its contents. Unlike the many medievalists associated with the Arts and Crafts, Mackmurdo admired Italian Renaissance and even Baroque architecture, and used the styles in his designs for several houses, including his own, Great Ruffins, in Essex. The furniture produced by the Guild was equally eclectic, ranging from the restrained and utilitarian to a style of decoration that anticipated the asymmetrical arabesques of the Aesthetic Movement and Art Nouveau. In fact, Mackmurdo associated with artists and literary figures connected with the cult of Aestheticism, artists of a quite different persuasion to many of those active in the craft guilds. Mackmurdo was an associate of J.A.M. Whistler and Oscar Wilde, both of whom had insisted upon the autonomy of the arts, that painting and design could be produced entirely for their own sake and need make no concession to social utility or the concerns of the audience. The party line among the crafts fraternity, by contrast, was often centred upon the social mission of art and its role to rescue the world from the ugliness of industry and capitalism. The catholic interests of the Century Guild and its ability to reconcile artists, architects and designers of a variety of persuasions, are evident in the contributors to *The Hobby Horse*. Editions of the Guild's magazine during its first years included contributions from Ruskin, Wilde, Rossetti, Paul Verlaine, Matthew Arnold, Herbert Gilchrist, W.S. Blunt, Selwyn Image and May Morris, covering items on art, literature and music.

BELOW Great Ruffins, Wickham Bishops, Essex, by Arthur Heygate Mackmurdo, c. 1904.
Mackmurdo, unlike other architects associated with the Arts and Crafts Movement, often admitted Renaissance, or in this instance Baroque, motifs into his building. Such sophisticated styles were anathema to William Morris.

RIGHT Frontispiece to Wren's City Churches by A.H. Mackmurdo, 1883.

FAR RIGHT Frontispiece for the Century Guild's magazine, The Hobby Horse.

BELOW RIGHT Oak writing desk by A.H. Mackmurdo, c. 1886.

61

RIGHT Church of All Saints, Leek, Staffordshire, by Gerald Horsley. Pen and watercolour, 1891.

The Century Guild was eventually dissolved in 1888. Although financially successful, many members of the Guild had pursued their own various interests. Horne, for example, continued his architectural practice and retired to Florence in 1900 to work as an art historian. Selwyn Image undertook independent work in several media, among them stained glass, typography, embroidery and mosaic, and Clement Heaton established his own business producing cloisonné enamel, later working in Europe and eventually settling in the United States. Mackmurdo continued his work as an architect and, like others in the Arts and Crafts Movement, strayed from work connected with the material fabric of society, its art, architecture and so on, to more theoretical concerns, in this instance monetary theory and sociology.

Selwyn Image, the co-founder of the Century Guild, was later active in another fraternity, the Art Workers' Guild. The Guild was established in 1884 and was, in part, formed from a group of young architects employed in the architect Richard Norman Shaw's practice, among them William Richard Lethaby – Shaw's chief clerk, Gerald Horsley, Ernest Newton, E.S. Prior and Mervyn Macartney. Encouraged by Shaw, his assistants were, like their counterparts in the Century Guild, interested in raising the status of the applied arts and breaching the division of labour that separated them from institutionalized notions of architecture and the fine arts of painting and sculpture that prevailed in the Royal Academy and at the Royal Institute of British Architects. In 1884 Shaw's assistants merged with a group of writers, designers and theorists known as 'The Fifteen', led by Lewis Forman Day. The Guild also included Walter Crane, John Sedding and Henry Holiday. The Art Workers' Guild shared most of the concerns of other Arts and Crafts ventures: it sought a handcrafted, well-designed environment in which artists, architects and craftsmen would assume collective responsibility for buildings and their contents. It is, however, difficult to discern within the Guild any clear sense of social purpose. The conspicuous radicalism that motivated the work of, say, Morris, is absent in the Art Workers' Guild. The Guild seems to have kept a deliberately low profile. It avoided controversy and in 1889 declared itself against 'public action', preferring, it seems, to influence the artistic establishment by stealth, for many of those active in the Guild were, over the next decade, to play prominent roles in art schools and public administration.

LEFT St Osmund's Church, Poole, Dorset, by E.S. Prior.

*RIGHT Perspective
drawing of Ernest
Newton's Fouracre at
West Green,
Hampshire, by Thomas
Hamilton Crawford,
1902.*

The Guild's reticence to maintain a public presence led in 1888 to the foundation of the affiliated but more militant Arts and Crafts Exhibition Society. The first members of the Society had been active either in the Art Workers' Guild or in business and were well known in the Arts and Crafts milieu. Crane, Webb, Benson, Cobden-Sanderson, Day, Lethaby and De Morgan were prominent in the Society and its exhibition accommodated the work of other like-minded guilds and crafts fraternities. The Society's first exhibition, held in the New Gallery in 1888, contained contributions both from its own members, from the Century Guild, Morris and Co. and C.R. Ashbee's nascent Guild and School of Handicraft. William De Morgan, active within the Society until 1906, exhibited a substantial amount of ceramic work, inspired by Islamic pottery, and W.A.S. Benson's hand-crafted metalwork was also well represented. Benson was a fierce critic not only of capitalist methods of mechanized production but also the equally capitalist methods of distribution through the medium of high street stores. He had established his own workshop in 1880 on Morris's advice, producing household products such as teapots and kettles in an often

simple style with clear evidence of the craftsman's handiwork left on the product. Society exhibitions over the next two years included submissions from Lethaby and Ernest Gimson, who, with D.J. Blow, had established a small shop in Bloomsbury for the sale of their own furniture, plaster and metalwork. Walter Crane, a regular exhibitor in a variety of media, re-asserted the radical calling of Arts and Crafts by exhibiting an Irish Nationalist Banner of his own design, and the Keswick School of Industrial Art submitted some characteristically simple examples of metalwork. In addition to providing a platform to exhibit a wide spectrum of crafts from an ever-expanding body of artisans, the Society's exhibitions also afforded the opportunity for theoretical discussions and practical demonstrations in a variety of crafts, including printing, bookbinding, design and tapestry weaving.

The Arts and Crafts Exhibition Society exhibited annually for the first three years. Thereafter it exhibited every three years. The quality of many of the submissions – particularly those by the London stores and the plethora of provincial guild fraternities and sororities that had been formed in the wake of Arts and Crafts ventures – was often poor. The

■

LEFT Sleeping
Beauty *wallpaper
designed by Walter
Crane.*

Society was, however, enormously influential in providing a platform for the exhibition of progressive design of a variety of aesthetic persuasions.

A more aggressively rustic style of furniture reminiscent of some of the first sorties into crafts made by the Pre-Raphaelites was evolved by Ernest Gimson and Sidney and Ernest Barnsley. Together with William Richard Lethaby, Reginald Blomfield and Mervyn Macartney, Gimson and Sidney Barnsley founded Kenton and Co. in 1890. The firm, which traded for less than two years, employed professional cabinetmakers to produce furniture to the designs of its founders, with each product carrying the initials of its maker. The style of Kenton and Co.'s work varies, although there is a marked return to some of the more simple and elegantly proportioned styles of the 18th century. After the company closed in 1892, Ernest Gimson, together with Sidney and Ernest Barnsley, moved to the Cotswolds, the first of many artists and craftsmen to settle in the district. The furniture designed around this period was unpretentious both in design and construction. The joinery is deliberately left visible and decoration is reduced to a minimum, a style that seems to have exasperated contemporary trade journals. A similar vernacular style permeated the architecture designed and built by Gimson and the Barnsleys. In fact, at Stoneywell in Markfield, Leicestershire, Ernest Gimson virtually succeeded in making vernacular architecture an organic part of the natural landscape. Built from materials such as uncut local stone and thatch, the elevation of this cottage literally follows the incline of the site on which it is built, with its massive chimney appearing to rise out of the landscape. Interior joinery forming the staircase and roof is equally simple, as was the rustic furniture designed for the cottage.

Another guild later to take up residence in the English Cotswolds was Charles Robert Ashbee's Guild and School of Handicraft. The Guild evolved from a Ruskin reading class held at Toynbee Hall in the East End of London under the direction of Ashbee, a Cambridge graduate and an associate of Morris and H.M. Hyndman. Whereas much of the produce of Arts and Crafts in the 1880s and 1890s had become increasingly eclectic in style and inten-tion, often employing highly refined standards of craftsmanship and, in some instances, mechanized production, Ashbee's Guild marked a distinct return to the Ruskinian and socialist principles that characterized the earlier work of the Arts and Crafts Movement. The product of one of the most lucid of the second generation of artists and craftsmen, Ashbee's declaration of the Arts and Crafts ideal is stirring stuff. In *Craftsmanship in Competitive Industry*, published in 1908, he stated:

The Arts and Crafts Movement ... assumes through its contact with the realities of life, an ethical significance of the greatest moment. It touches both producer and consumer alike, and so it touches everybody. It brings ... into modern industry a little of that Soul, that imaginative quality in which our civilisation is so lacking. It reminds us that the imaginative things are real things, and shows us that when they are expressed in man's handiwork, they must come into immediate contact with material actuality.

What I seek to show is that this Arts and Crafts movement, which began with the earnestness of the Pre-Raphaelite Painters, the prophetic enthusiasm of Ruskin and the Titanic energy of Morris is not what the public has thought it to be, or is seeking to make it: a nursery for luxuries, a hothouse for the production of mere trivialities and useless things for the rich. It is a movement for the stamping out of such things by sound production on the one hand, and the inevitable regulation of machine production and cheap labour on the other.

The shoddy practice of industrialized production had been stamped out on several fronts. Ashbee insisted that crafts should be self-taught, the skill of the craftsman gradually evolving as his familiarity with the medium increased. He deliberately recruited unskilled workers in preference to tradesmen, educating them through the Guild's classes. Labour within the Guild workshops was undivided, with each craftsman involved with the whole production process. There was an emphasis on handicraft – 'the winged spirit we want to embody', wrote Ashbee, 'flies away at the touch of a duplicating machine'. Moreover, Guild members were encouraged to work cooperatively, each one in appreciation of the strengths and weaknesses of his or her comrades. In 1898, when the Guild became financially stable, Ashbee limited the liability of the company and offered his employees representation on the company's newly formed board.

OPPOSITE Design for a dado by Walter Crane.

RIGHT The Magpie and Stump by C.R. Ashbee in Cheyne Walk, Chelsea, London. The design and decoration of the house attracted the attention of The Studio *magazine and of the German Hermann Muthesius, author of* Das Englische Haus.

OPPOSITE ABOVE Sketchbook design for a ladderback chair by Ernest Gimson.

OPPOSITE BELOW Ladderback chair in ash by Ernest Gimson, c. 1895.

He also started a scheme in which a percentage could be deducted from the wages of his employees to give them a financial interest in the Guild.

The work produced by the Guild was simple in design. Its metalwork, in the form of jewellery, cutlery, plates and vases, was often inspired by medieval sources, with the addition of semiprecious stones and modest decorative devices similar in appearance to Art Nouveau. Ashbee, however, disliked the association and saw a marked distinction between the high socialist and craft ideals of the Guild and the self-consciously artistic sensibilities of the Art Nouveau products that permeated fashionable high street stores. Equally simple was the furniture produced by the Guild. Cabinets were usually constructed from oak or walnut, with large masses of unadorned wood offset by decorative metal handles and hinges. In fact, a late example of the Guild's cabinetmaking, shown at the Arts and Crafts Exhibition of 1896, had virtually all of its surface decoration removed, a style that was increasingly to dominate turn-of-the-century design.

In 1902 the fortunes of the Guild and School of Handicraft changed after it moved from its workshops at Essex House in the East End of London to Chipping Campden in Gloucestershire. The countryside was a more appropriate setting for a craft fraternity and Ashbee established workshops in the rundown village with some 50 of his craftsmen and their families. He offered the residents of Chipping Campden – few of whom warmed to his overtures – classes in his Campden School of Arts and Crafts, a counterpart to the educational programme offered in London. The curriculum included lectures by Walter Crane, among others, and practical instruction in subjects such as needlework, gardening, physical education and starching laundry. By 1905 the Guild's finances were looking precarious, with the year's business returning a loss of almost one thousand pounds, a loss that was virtually doubled during the following year. A manager was appointed to run the business and attempts were made to raise capital from shareholders, but the company eventually went into voluntary liquidation. The reasons for the Guild's demise were thought to be various. In a letter to his shareholders, Ashbee partly attributed the Guild's downfall to its

38-39 CHEYNE WALK
CHELSEA : S·W·

C·R·ASHBEE·MA·ARCHITE
MAGPIE & STUMP HOUSE: B
37 CHEYNE WALK·CHELS

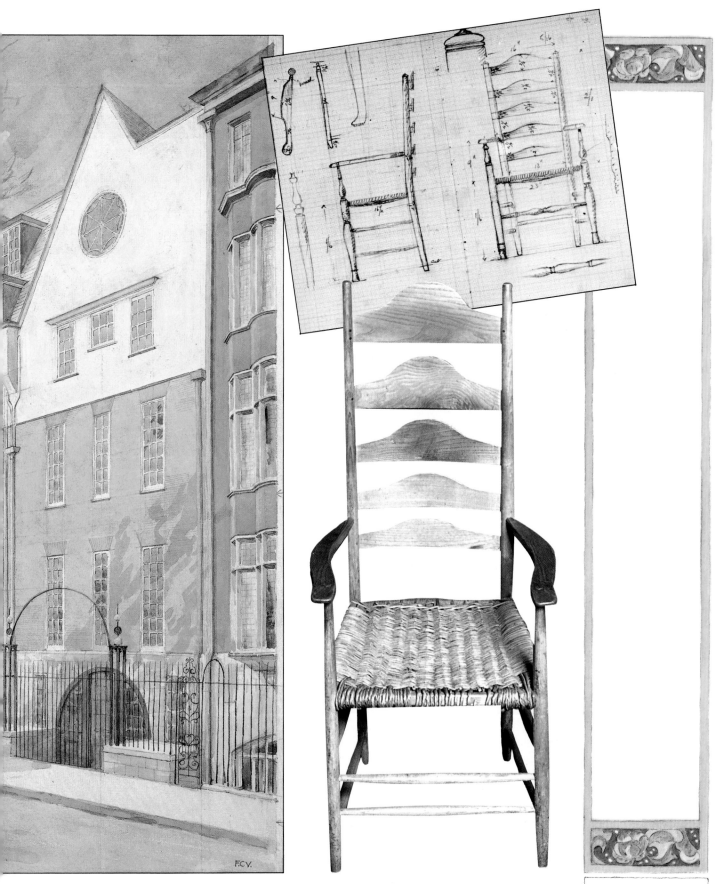

location. Craftsmen were unable to find alternative work in the countryside when orders declined and the cost of operating a business remote from urban markets was prohibitive. The problems were further exacerbated by the mechanized techniques used by market competitors. The Arts and Crafts style had become very fashionable by the turn of the century, although few of those that exploited its appearance felt it necessary to apply the same high standards of workmanship. Ashbee, nonetheless, struck a defiant note in the letter written to shareholders in the company on the eve of its collapse, defending the ideals of the enterprise and its achievements.

From the financial point of view, the Guild and School of Handicraft had failed. In *Craftmanship and Competitive Industry*, Ashbee presented an astute interpretation of its failure. He wrote: 'and since it has definitely been shown that it is impractical to carry on the arts and crafts upon any large scale, under existing industrial conditions, we must set to and devise other ways in which the work we want to do can be done'. Not for the first time had well-intentioned socialist craftsmen met head on with the megalith of industrial capitalism.

The Guild and School of Handicraft had

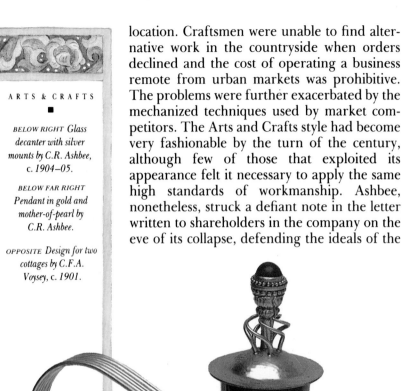

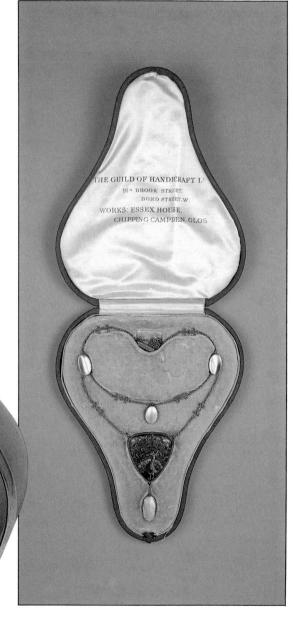

made various complaints against unfair competition, be it from mechanized industry or amateur sororities undercutting the Guild by failing to charge for their labour. Guilds such as those of Ashbee and Mackmurdo were, by the last decades of the 19th century, no longer operating in isolation. Beautifully produced handmade products, as contemporary art magazines such as the *Art Journal* and *The Studio* indicate, had permeated the public consciousness. Liberty and Co. had distributed Arts and Crafts products to a wider clientele and the demand for and interest in Arts and Crafts had risen accordingly.

At the lower end of the social scale, the Home Arts and Industries Association, established in 1884, had sought to protect country crafts and traditions and to encourage rural workers to put their leisure time to good use. The Association, a charitable body, was run on the whole by upper middle-class women and had the patronage of the local aristocracy. Its aim had been to raise standards of aesthetic taste and afford ailing parts of the rural economy an alternative source of income through the Victorian ideal of self-help. The Association was founded by one Mrs Jebb, with the support of A.H. Mackmurdo, and taught metal- and woodwork, together with knitting, embroidery and spinning. Women workers, largely absent in the more famous crafts guilds, at least as shop-floor producers, were common in the Association both as local organizers and workers. The Association had helped distribute the work of a number of smaller provincial crafts guilds and adult-education associations, among them the Keswick School of Industrial Art, a small design school established in Cumberland, in 1884, and which was eventually to sustain itself as a business venture through the sale of its work. Another sorority motivated by a patrician concern for the poor was the Royal School of Needlework, established in Kensington, London, to help women in distressed circumstances to earn a living from needlework. Some idea of the nature of the school was given by Tiffany's associate, the American fabric designer Candace Wheeler. Visiting England prior to establishing her own counterpart to the Kensington School, she is recorded as being shocked to see the vivid class divisions between the benign middle-class organizers and the women workers.

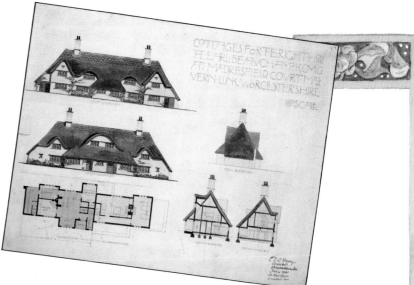

Women workers were also instrumental, as Anthea Callen observes, in the revival of the Langdale linen industry, founded in Langley, Cumberland, around 1885. The work of the Industry is eulogized in the 1897 edition of the *Art Journal*. Picturesque but sturdy homes contain a welcoming kitchen complete with an open fire over which a kettle boils. The scene 'once common throughout England but now an object for curiosity in shops and museums', could, at first glance, spring from any Arts and Crafts vision of socialist Utopia, but, in this instance, the craft revival is depicted as a model of a Victorian obsession with cleanliness, hard work and self-discipline as the antidote to poverty. The industry 'has brought increased comfort and orderliness into many a home, whose mistress is now to be found busily engaged by her own fireside instead of gossiping beside a neighbour's', the writer (a woman) stated. She continued:

When cottage mothers are engaged in the production of really beautiful fabrics, the whole family must benefit, thereby learning unconsciously to appreciate beautiful things, and also receiving a much needed training in conscientious work, no mean advantage in these days of scamping.

The original craft ideal had been turned on its head as public interest in the beautiful and handmade grew. Resonant Victorian themes of hard work, thrift and a benign and deserving poor upstaged the idealism of the movement by embracing the form of the Arts and Crafts but nothing of its socialist and democratic content. Women of little visible wealth communally producing handicrafts of excep-

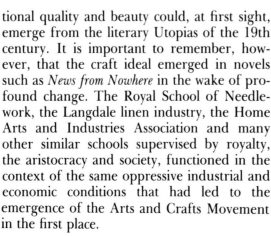

tional quality and beauty could, at first sight, emerge from the literary Utopias of the 19th century. It is important to remember, however, that the craft ideal emerged in novels such as *News from Nowhere* in the wake of profound change. The Royal School of Needlework, the Langdale linen industry, the Home Arts and Industries Association and many other similar schools supervised by royalty, the aristocracy and society, functioned in the context of the same oppressive industrial and economic conditions that had led to the emergence of the Arts and Crafts Movement in the first place.

If the Victorian craft schools turned the craft ideal on its head in one direction, the efforts of Arthur Lasenby Liberty did so in another. His by no means insignificant contribution to the Arts and Crafts Movement will be considered in greater detail below, although in this instance it is interesting to note that the craft ideal was modified not by the exploitation of manual labour but by the exploitation of markets and machinery. Originally established in 1875, Liberty and Co. managed to produce and distribute couture, fabrics, metalwork and furniture to a wider public than that for which Morris and his followers worked. The indivi-

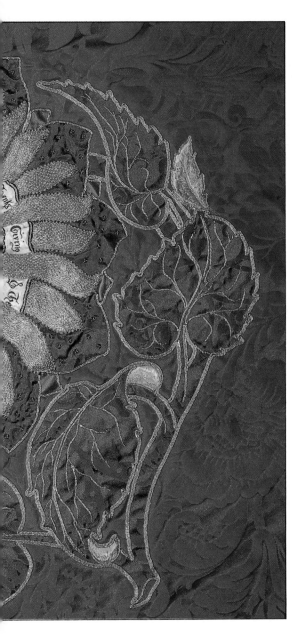

dual handicraft and creative expression of the artisans, the majority of whom worked anonymously, disappeared, to be replaced by a coalition with manufacturers who produced goods mechanically at a fraction of the cost of competitors. It is significant that C.R. Ashbee took exception to the cheap labour of poor amateurs and mechanical production, for both afforded a quick and easy route to the exterior appearance of the craft ideal. Absent on both accounts, however, was the radical change in social conditions that would enable the arts and crafts to be humanely made and enjoyed by the whole of society.

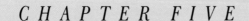

CHAPTER FIVE

THE CRAFT IDEAL IN THE UNITED STATES

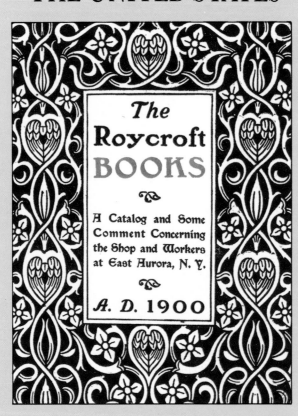

*Frontispiece to a book produced by the Roycroft Press, founded by
Elbert Hubbard.*

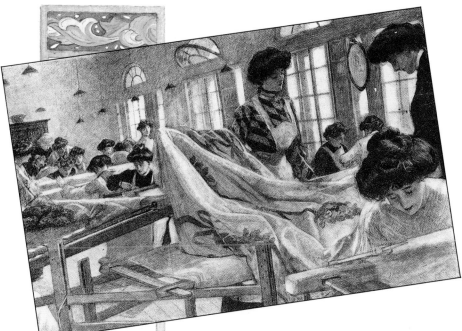

ABOVE *View of the Royal School of Needlework's workroom in 1904.*

bust of a young woman sculpted to order in butter in less than two hours.

Interest in the Arts and Crafts Movement in the United States was, for the most part, inspired by British contributors to the exhibition. Richard Norman Shaw, from whose studio the Art Workers' Guild had in part emerged, exhibited several influential designs for buildings in the 'Queen Anne' style. Shaw's vernacular building bore something of a resemblance to a colonial style and had a strong appeal to architects eager to abandon not only the classical style but also the equally European Gothic idiom. There was, independent of Shaw's influence, a developing additional interest in America's colonial past. *Harper's Magazine* had recently included articles on colonial architecture, and the Centennial Exposition contained a tableau of a kitchen from the period before the Revolution. It was from this network of influences, both homespun and foreign, that a vernacular style of architecture developed, known as the 'Shingle style'. Architects such as William Ralph Emerson, H.H. Richardson, and firms such as McKim, Mead and White rejected many of the more obviously mainstream European influences in building and returned to a rustic, timber-built colonial idiom. Richardson had adopted this vernacular Shingle style around 1880 in preference to the classical manner he had acquired in France as a student and, in keeping with the work of British Arts and Crafts architects, assumed responsibility not only for the exterior of the building but also its contents. The office of H.H. Richardson produced examples of simple furniture designed, in most cases, by assistants and made by professional contractors.

Equally important in the evolution of an American craft ideal were the other British Arts and Crafts exhibits at Philadelphia. Jeffrey and Co. – the firm that had printed Morris's first wallpapers, Fairfax Murray, Walter Crane and the Royal School of Needlework had all contributed to the exhibition. In addition, the work, and to a lesser extent the ideals, of Morris were becoming increasingly well known in the United States. The company's ironwork and versions of his Sussex chair were commercially distributed and a number of designers confessed to having been influenced by his example.

 Contact between the British Arts and Crafts Movement and artists, architects and designers in the United States was, at first, limited. The work of Downing, Renwick and Jarves had been influenced by the revival of a Gothic style in Britain in the late 19th century and Ruskin's writing had been enthusiastically received by some American painters and critics. A more substantial grasp of the Arts and Crafts Movement and its possible application to American culture did not really occur, however, until the Centennial Exposition held in Philadelphia in 1876.

The exhibition demonstrated the economic and political virility of the United States as the home of private enterprise and liberal democracy. It was apparent, however, that in the spheres of art, architecture and the decorative arts, the United States had yet to fashion a culture of its own. While a few notable and original examples of American work were included in the exhibition – Shaker furniture and the work of various Cincinnati potters, for instance – the majority of the industrial arts was dominated by the novel and decorative machine-produced Empire style so criticized by Downing. American popular taste for novelty perhaps achieved its apotheosis in the Centennial Exposition in the form of the

LOUIS C TIFFANY & ASSOCIATED ARTISTS

One such designer who claimed to be influenced by Morris was Louis Comfort Tiffany (1848–1933). Tiffany had established Louis C. Tiffany and Associated Artists in 1879 with Lockwood de Forest, Samuel Colman and Candace Wheeler. They had planned to run a studio following the example of a Renaissance workshop, with Tiffany as the creative centre surrounded by assistants working in a variety of media. The company worked mainly in the fields of glass and fabric design; its original purpose was to establish an alliance between art and industry and to revive standards of domestic taste in the United States. Despite Tiffany's ambitions, his company had few parallels with Morris's experiment. Tiffany never established any clear idea about the way in which art might combat philistinism and appears to have operated, like some designers on the other side of the Atlantic, on the general understanding that art was indiscriminately good for society. The exact mechanics of the conditions under which art was produced and consumed, the very stuff of Morris's concerns, were not considered. Tiffany's venture was nonetheless commercially very success-

ful and the company quickly acquired prestigious commissions, not least of which was the contract to decorate the White House for President Chester A. Arthur. The company split early in the next decade, with Tiffany and Wheeler working independently, the one trading as Louis C. Tiffany and Co. and the other (Wheeler) as Associated Artists. Louis C. Tiffany's work is well documented. Less well known, and more germane to the Arts and Crafts tradition in the United States, was the

BELOW Examples of glass produced by Louis C. Tiffany between 1890 and the 1920s. Tiffany's firm, although without Tiffany's direct involvement, continued to produce glass until 1938.

work of his associate. Candace Wheeler had, following the example of the Royal School of Needlework, established the Society of Decorative Art in New York, which became the model for other sororities in Philadelphia and Boston. Among the aims of the Society was to represent a craft with which women had traditionally been associated not as some domestic pastime but as an activity that reflected what Wheeler understood to be women's innate creativity and sense of design.

ABOVE Photograph of Candace Wheeler, one of the most prominent designers in the American Arts and Crafts Movement.

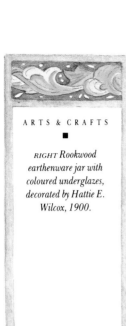

RIGHT Rookwood earthenware jar with coloured underglazes, decorated by Hattie E. Wilcox, 1900.

One of the most conspicuous developments in American Arts and Crafts – and one developed again by craftswomen rather than men – occurred in the field of ceramics. In Cincinnati a group of socially prominent women amateurs attended the city's School of Art and rapidly became equally prominent in their field, exhibiting at the 1876 Women's Pavilion at Philadelphia, where their work was also used for the Centennial tea party. One student from the Cincinnati school, Mary Louise McLaughlin, was particularly influential. In 1879 McLaughlin, who also claimed to have been influenced by the example of William Morris, established The Cincinnati Pottery Club with Clara Chapman Newton and evolved what became a characteristically American style of decoration based on a French technique of ceramic underglazing first seen by McLaughlin at the Centennial's French Pavilion.

The same technique was used by McLaughlin's contemporary, Maria Longworth Nichols, the founder of the Rookwood Pottery. Rookwood (the name was meant to evoke Wedgwood) was founded in 1880 by Nichols with money given by her father, a dealer in real estate and a local phil anthropist in the arts.

Maria Longworth Nichols claimed, as Anthea Callen observes, that Rookwood had been established mainly for her own gratification, although the venture was both large and financially successful. Some idea of the scale of the pottery is given when one considers that Rookwood absorbed a number of craftsmen from local industries to throw the clay for the mainly female contingent of decorators. The year after its formation, Rookwood lent its facilities to a number of skilled women amateurs and began supporting classes in ceramics. Tuition was offered (at the very expensive rate of three dollars per week) with the aim of training prospective ceramicists for the firm. The project was abandoned, however, on the advice of Rookwood's business manager, W.W. Taylor, on the grounds that the company was openly fostering competition in its own field. The pottery's excellent facilities were denied to the very skilled ceramicists connected with the Pottery Club and Rookwood had a virtual monopoly on underglazing, a difficult technique requiring mild firing to maintain the characteristic warm-coloured glazes. After her second marriage Maria Longworth Storer, continued to practise as a potter but left the running of Rookwood to Taylor.

The company continued, however, and trained an impressive stable of both male and female ceramicists, among them Shirayamandi, one of the company's few foreign craftsmen, Artus Van Briggle, Laura Fry and Matthew Daly.

The notion that creative work enabled women to turn their hands to a useful trade appropriate to their sex was one that occurred on the periphery of the Arts and Crafts Movement time and again. In the United States it appears in the Paul Revere Pottery in Boston, where classes were held for immigrant women workers, and in the Newcomb College Pottery attached to the women's section of Tulane University in New Orleans. The Newcomb College Pottery was established in 1895 and at first attempted to imitate the work of Rookwood, although it found the specialist glazing techniques too difficult to copy. Under the direction of Mary G. Sheerer, Newcomb began to evolve its own peculiar style based upon not only the use of local clays but also local decorative plant motifs common to the Southern states. A sense of geographical identity is very common in American crafts and appeared in Susan Frackelton's work at Newcomb, which evolved from a style peculiar to her native Wisconsin.

The demand for and interest in Art Pottery appeared to be nationwide. The

Chelsea Keramic Art Works in Massachusetts had produced traditional pottery since its foundation in 1866, and after the Centennial Exposition began to produce work influenced by Japanese and French ceramics. Lustre and matt glazes were the speciality of Clara Louise Poillon's Pottery, established in 1901, and the Boston-based Grueby Faience Co., which evolved a simple form of pottery decorated in a distinctive matt green glaze. Research indicates that the United States made a distinct contribution to the field of pottery, yet despite the 'good works' of Candace Wheeler, Newcomb College and the Paul Revere Pottery, the missionary zeal associated with creative labour that is so resonant within the British Arts and Crafts tradition is largely absent in most examples of American ceramics. American pottery is often aesthetically very pleasing, although it is never really used as a vehicle to challenge the artistic or social status quo. The zeal absent in the work of most American art potters appeared with a vengeance toward the end of the 19th century with the Rose Valley Association near Philadelphia, an artistic community that had tried to embrace not just the visible part of the craft ideal but also aspects of its socialism. In 1901 two architects, William L. Price and H.H. McLanahan, had attempted to establish a fraternity outside Philadelphia in disused mill buildings.

LEFT Vase produced by the Paul Revere Pottery, Boston, after 1908.

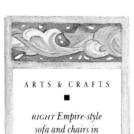

■

RIGHT Empire-style sofa and chairs in laminated rosewood and white pine by John Henry Belter, c. 1855.

Modelled on the communal ideals practised by Morris and Ashbee in England, the community was partly supported by Swarthmore College. Craftsmen from Switzerland were used to train local labour and the Association made pottery and furniture distributed through a retail outlet in Philadelphia. The Association foundered after eight years, apparently beset by the same problems of the cost of handcraftsmanship that dogged the many other idealistic Arts and Crafts communities. However, the craft ideal appears in far more robust form in the example of Gustav Stickley.

Gustav Stickley had originally been apprenticed to Schuler C. Brandt, his maternal uncle. After managing Brandt's small furniture factory, Stickley began to produce work of his own. His earliest examples of furniture appear to have met the popular demand for reproductions of European styles, although these were apparently done under duress. 'At first', Stickley wrote, 'in obedience to public demand, I produced in my workshops adaptations of foreign styles, but always under silent protest; my opposition developing, as I believe, out of a course of reading, largely from Ruskin and Emerson which I followed in my youth'. Stickley thought that the popular taste for European-inspired furniture was theatrical and out of context when applied to American homes. He understood that the European styles were peculiar to individual national identities, growing out of their own respective cultures. He considered it anomalous to take, say, the Empire style, which was the adequate expression of the aspirations of 19th-century France, and transport it to the other side of the Atlantic where its historical and social context would be lost. The excesses of the ornate Empire style were an easy target for criticism,

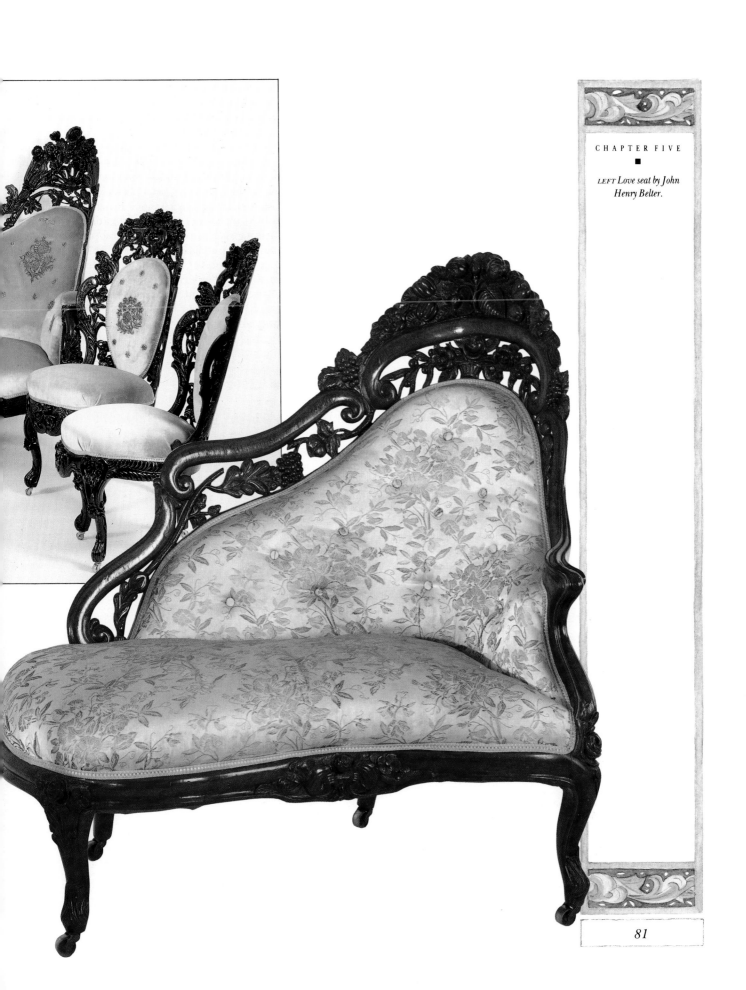

but Stickley rejected not just these but also the stylistic alternatives current in the late 19th century, including Japonisme, Gothic revival and even the work of the Modern Movement. Stickley's remedy was to abandon any influence motivated by appearance alone. 'I became convinced', he wrote 'that the designers of cabinet making use their eyes and their memories too freely and their reasoning powers too little'. The style, or more properly, the method Stickley used in cabinetmaking, he dubbed 'Structural'. This was a functional and austere style, similar in character to the Shaker furniture he had seen at the Philadelphia Centennial Exposition, and devoid of virtually any form of decoration.

Whereas individual styles of Empire, Gothic or Modern furniture represented various strands of European national culture, Stickley's aggressively simple furniture became an expression of American aesthetic values expressed in American terms. The furniture was made well but was simple and unpretentious. Constructed from humble, local materials, usually oak, it was inexpensive and within the reach of the average American consumer. Moreover, the furniture owed no stylistic debts

to European models. Such independence and straightforward 'common-sense' resonate through American culture. Stickley stated:

They [the Americans] are the great middle classes, possessed of moderate culture and moderate material resources, modest in schemes and action, average in all but virtues. Called upon to meet stern issues, they have remaining little leisure in which to study problems of other and milder nature. But as offering such great and constant service, these same middle classes should be the objects of solicitude in all that makes for their comfort, their pleasure and mental development. For them art should not be allowed to remain as a subject of consideration for critics. It should be brought to their homes and become for them a part and parcel of their daily lives. A simple, democratic art should provide them with the material surroundings conducive to plain living and high thinking, to the development of the sense of order, symmetry and proportion.

Stickley gave attention both to the form of his furniture and the manner in which it was made. He set great store by Morris's demand that the labour of the craftsman should be free and contented. To this end his firm of United Craftsmen attempted to evoke the communal

fraternities of the Middle Ages. Stickley even adopted a medieval device, *Als Ich Kan,* taken from the painting of the 15th-century artist Jan Van Eyck and used in its English translation – If I Can – in some of the works of William Morris. Stickley's craftsmen were also incorporated into a profit-sharing scheme and regular meetings were held at the workshops, where 'friendly debate, brief addresses and genial discussion will be used as methods to secure harmony and unity of effort.' Machinery was used in the workshops, but only to liberate the craftsman from unnecessary work.

The aims of United Craftsmen were catalogued in the company's magazine, *The Craftsman,* published for the first time in 1901. The first edition was dedicated to Morris and subsequently contained contributions on the Arts and Crafts from both sides of the Atlantic, together with a cross-section of liberal critical essays on subjects from Native American songs to Art Nouveau. Later editions of the magazine increased in size and format and included articles by Stickley on education and social reform, an interest that found form in Craftsman Farms, a working agricultural venture under Stickley's direction wherein a school for

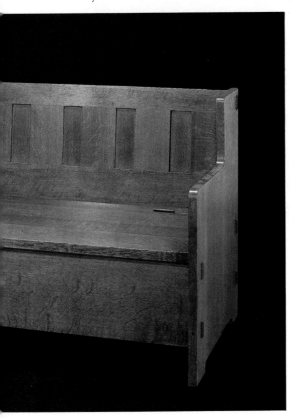

boys was established to supplement the shortcomings of traditional academic education.

In the first decade of the 20th century United Craftsmen appeared to go from strength to strength. In 1902 the company took larger premises in Syracuse, where workshops and showrooms adjoined a library and a lecture hall. Metalwork and fabric were produced in addition to woodwork. Three years later Stickley's furniture was being widely imitated under trade names deceptively similar to United Craftsmen. The name was accordingly changed, first to United Crafts and later to Craftsmen Incorporated and the company moved to New York, where showrooms, a permanent exhibition, a lecture hall, a library, the equivalent to a modern supermarket and a restaurant were centralized in a large twelve-storey building. The rapid growth of the company caused its decline and eventual collapse. Its assets were gradually stripped and Stickley's interest in the company was terminated. Despite an ignominious end, United Craftsmen represented a radical departure in the American Arts and Crafts Movement. Stickley had followed not simply the outward signs of craftsmanship but also the spirit. The work was pleasing to look at, well and sensibly made by creatively fulfiled craftsmen who were getting something like proper remuneration for their labour. Moreover, Stickley's products owed no stylistic debt to European influences, save that of notions of common-sense craftsmanship pioneered originally by Ruskin and Morris. United Craftsmen furniture thereby became a fitting medium to reflect the modest democratic ideals of American citizenship.

LEFT Photographs published in The Craftsman *of Gustav Stickley's Craftsman Workshops, c. 1902–03.*

BELOW LEFT Oak hall bench produced by Gustav Stickley, c. 1910.

*LEFT Artist's
impression of a
Craftsman House, one
of a series of homes in
an American
vernacular style
published in* The
Craftsman, *1904.*

*BELOW LEFT Artist's
impression of a dining
room, published in*
The Craftsman,
1904.

The Arts and Crafts ideal was applied with equal enthusiasm (if not equal reverence) by Stickley's contemporary Elbert Hubbard. Hubbard, in his own words educated at the University of Hard Knocks (his presence there is noted in *Who's Who*), originally made a living as a travelling salesman and later tried his hand, with little initial success, at writing novels. The lack of enthusiasm shown by local publishers was however put to good use. Hubbard was later to sponsor the *Philistine*, one of numerous and usually short-lived pocket-sized magazines with the sole aim of settling a few scores with those editors too blind or stupid to appreciate his literary talents. The magazine ran for a number of years, returning a profit from its very first edition.

Hubbard's foray into the Arts and Crafts Movement had been inspired by the Kelmscott Press. He had met Ruskin and Morris in England in 1894 and set up a press at East Aurora on his return to New York. The Roycroft Press took its name from two English bookbinders of the 17th century, Samuel and Thomas Roycroft. The venture began with the publication of one book, the first of a long series of biographical essays written by Hubbard, entitled *Little Journeys,* the

Journey in this instance being to the home of George Eliot. Many of the first books produced at Roycroft were very lavish. The typeface had been designed in imitation of 17th-century-style lettering, printed using a hand press on handmade paper imported from Europe and finally bound in leather. Some editions contained decorative borders and a few early examples were even illuminated by hand.

In 1901 Roycroft began producing earnest-looking, Mission-style furniture similar to that produced at United Craftsmen, together with equally simple ceramics and household items in metal. Some examples were produced in brass or silver, although Roycroft was better known for its hand-beaten copperware, often made to the designs of the ex-banker-turned-artisan Karl Kipp.

ABOVE *Illustrated frontispiece to* Little Journeys to the Homes of English Authors, *one of a series published by Elbert Hubbard, 1901.*

LEFT *Print of the Roycroft Shops at Hubbard's crafts community in East Aurora, near Buffalo, New York.*

ABOVE RIGHT *Photograph of Elbert Hubbard.*

RIGHT *Frontispiece from* Little Journeys to the Homes of Great Teachers *by Elbert Hubbard, 1908.*

CHAPTER FIVE
■

*LEFT One of a series of
devices used by Gustav
Stickley with the motto
Als ich Kan.*

Like United Craftsmen, Roycroft had democratic pretensions; its catalogue proudly declared that beautiful objects should be available to everyone. Hubbard had hoped to be able to encourage his craftsmen to work without the aid of machinery although, like countless other craftsmen, he found that the well-intentioned aim of pricing household goods within the reach of the average income was incompatible with the aim of respecting the creative integrity of the artisan. Hubbard, like others active in the Arts and Crafts Movement in the United States, compromised by using mechanized processess. However, despite such heresies, he gave great attention to the working practices and conditions at East Aurora. Individual craftsmen, where possible, maintained a considerable degree of autonomy in their daily work. Examples of Roycroft furniture tended to be individually made by one craftsman, and apprentices, having mastered one craft, were encouraged to move to another to further develop their skills. Extending the medieval guild system to characteristically extreme limits, Hubbard dubbed himself 'Fra Hubbard', the leader of a putative band of brothers recruited in the main from the locality around East Aurora.

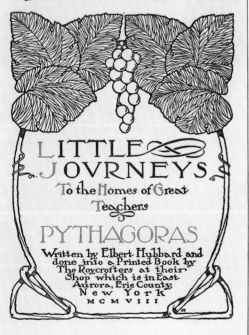

RIGHT Robie House,
Chicago, by Frank
Lloyd Wright, 1908.

One of the principal features of the American Arts and Crafts Movement evident in the work of both Stickley and Hubbard was its increasing ability to be able to compromise with mechanized production. In England, where the Industrial Revolution had created social conditions comparable to the urban lifestyles of some of today's Third World countries, it is easy to appreciate the fear generated by mechanization. The United States, however, was not witness to anything comparable to the social changes that occurred in England, and welcomed the creative possibilities of machine production. One of the chief figures responsible for assimilating the ideals of the Arts and Crafts Movement with those of mechanized production was the architect and designer Frank Lloyd Wright.

Wright trained as an architect in the offices of Joseph Silsbee and the firm of Adler and Sullivan. His first architectural designs were in the 'Prairie' style and on first sight appear to have little in common with Arts and Crafts architecture in England. Wright's buildings nonetheless observe some important aspects of the Arts and Crafts canon. Morris had insisted upon an honesty anticipating the modern preoccupation with 'truth to material' and suggested that buildings should be an intrinsic part of their environment. Members of the second generation of the movement in England had, in addition, insisted upon the relationship between the design of the building and its contents. All of these features are evident in Wright's work, the principal difference being that the geography of the Cotswolds was exchanged for that of the prairies of Illinois. The

buildings of the Prairie School consequently stress flat, open geography by constantly drawing attention to the horizontal dimension of the architecture with the use of low overhanging roofs and water tables that extend well beyond the walls of the house. Overhanging roofs were not simply matters of stylistic caprice – they afforded excellent protection from the extremes in weather conditions. The height of each individual storey, in turn, was determined by the scale of the human figure. Wright had also sought to reconcile the design of the exterior of his buildings with furniture and household items, ambitions shared by his contemporaries Greene and Greene, active mainly on the West Coast.

Wright had first come into contact with the

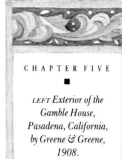

CHAPTER FIVE
■
*LEFT Exterior of the
Gamble House,
Pasadena, California,
by Greene & Greene,
1908.*

Arts and Crafts Movement through the works
of Ruskin, and in 1898 became one of the
founding members of the Chicago Arts and
Crafts Society. Chicago was, in fact, an active
centre for arts and crafts. Hull House, a settle-
ment under the direction of social reformer
Jane Addams, included an art gallery and
studio and was inspired by London's Toynbee
Hall (Ashbee and Crane both had connections
with Hull House). In addition, Chicago maintained a William Morris Society, established by
Joseph Twyman, and the Industrial Art
League, under the direction of Oscar Lovell
Triggs, was designed to promote Arts and
Crafts ideals. Wright distinguished himself
from other craftsmen in the city by his attitude
to machine production. Triggs, for example,

had reservations about mechanized industry
and thought that beauty was contingent upon
the human hand. Wright, however, saw the
creative, technical and social possibilities
afforded by machinery. The division that
separated the factions in the Chicago Arts and
Crafts Society was not that which divided
Ruskin and Morris from the capitalist industrialists of the mid-19th century. Rather, the
issue concerned the extent to which men and
women could control the machine and the way
in which it could be used to make good and
affordable items. Wright maintained that
properly deployed machines could produce
objects that were simple and truthful to their
respective materials, criteria demanded by the
Arts and Crafts Movement decades earlier. In

addition, he pointed out that mechanized processes had also been used to turn out 'machine-made copies of handicraft originals', pale and ludicrous imitations of the Empire style – 'the whole mass a tortured sprawl supposed artistic'. Machinery, used with intelligence, had the capacity to show wood in a more truthful and flattering light; not as a phoney work of machine-made 'handicraft' but as something simply but well turned out, using the machine as a logical tool. Wright stated his position in a famous lecture given at Hull House, entitled 'The Art and Craft of the Machine'. 'American Society', Wright said, 'has the essential tool of its own age by the blade, as lacerated hands everywhere testify!' He continued:

The machines used in woodwork will show that by unlimited power in cutting, shaping and smoothing, and by the tireless repeat, they have emancipated beauties of wood-nature, making possible without waste, beautiful surface treatments, clean and strong forms that veneers of Sheraton or Chippendale only hinted at with dire extravagance. Beauty unknown even to the middle ages. These machines have undoubtedly placed within reach of the designer a technique enabling him to realize the true nature of wood in his designs harmoniously with man's sense of beauty, satisfying his material needs with such extraordinary economy as to put this beauty of wood in use within the reach of everyone.

Wright, in many respects, compromised and renegotiated the ideals of the Arts and Crafts with the pressing demands of the Machine Age, and did much to wean the movement from an obsessive and unrealistic concern with the hand-made. The *bête noire* of mechanization was introduced into the prospectus of the Arts and Crafts, a move that was anathema to the movement. It is, however, important to recognize that one of the long-standing democratic aims of the Arts and Crafts Movement was to place inexpensive but well-designed products within the range of the common man, and this could only be achieved with methods of production that were less costly than handcraftsmanship. Perhaps Wright's most significant achievement was to accept this compromise and re-invent a concern for truth to material with the machine as an integral part of the process. Machinery simply became another tool in the hands of the craftsman, an ideal that was to be subsequently developed by the German craft workshops.

CHAPTER FIVE
■

*LEFT Dining room of
the Gamble House by
Greene & Greene.*

*BELOW LEFT Armchair
by Frank Lloyd Wright.*

THE AESTHETIC BACKDROP

*Numbers 5 and 7 Blenheim Road, Bedford Park, London, two of a
substantial number of houses on the estate designed by Richard
Norman Shaw.*

RIGHT Sideboard in the Japanese style designed by E.W. Godwin and made by William Wyatt, c. 1867.

 For the majority of craftsmen and women referred to so far, the Arts and Crafts were seen as a vehicle for change or reform, and implicated a host of historical, political, social and cultural ideas and opinions. However, relatively few of the observers of the artistic scene would have been aware of the lofty aims of the Arts and Crafts Movement. 'Art' had suddenly become very fashionable among the upper middle classes, and the patrons of Arthur Lasenby Liberty's Regent Street store or the residents of Richard Norman Shaw's Bedford Park, in London, would have embraced all things 'artistic' irrespective of their theoretical pedigree. In the latter part of the 19th century, styles such as the Gothic, the Japoniste or the aggressively modern Art Nouveau current in Europe appear to have been received with equal and uncritical enthusiasm. Art had, as the painter J.A.M. Whistler observed, become a common topic for the tea table.

Art had initially become a popular subject for conversation among the upper middle classes through the influence of high street stores. A number of these had opened in the 1870s selling fashionable fabrics and *objets d'art* inspired by or imported from the Orient. Stores such as Debenham's and Swan and Edgar sold fabrics, and the designer Christopher Dresser had visited Japan in 1877 and opened a warehouse of Japanese imported goods.

By far the most important vehicle bringing art to the tea table was Arthur Lasenby Liberty's store, opened in London's Regent

BELOW LEFT Liberty and Co.'s bamboo bookcase lined with gold leather paper, from the firm's illustrated catalogue.

BELOW RIGHT Bamboo folding card table, produced by Liberty and Co.

CENTRE RIGHT Wallpaper design by C.F.A. Voysey, one of a number of floral paper and fabric designs produced after Voysey established his own architectural practice in 1882.

Street in 1875. Liberty sold fashionable imported silk from the Orient, Japanese blue-and-white porcelain and furniture inspired by oriental models. Its products proved immediately popular and later other items were sold, including furniture, fabrics, clothes, metalware, carpets and pottery. The store boasted an impressive list of craftsmen. Archibald Knox designed the famous Celtic-inspired 'Cymric' and 'Tudric' metalwares and Walter Crane and C.F.A. Voysey were associated with some of Liberty's fabrics. George Walton designed much of its furniture, and couture was produced and sold under the supervision of the architect E.W. Godwin. Many of the craftsmen and women active for the store worked without attribution. Their designs were often modified, and mechanized techniques were used to produce goods in quantity. Liberty had ridden roughshod over many aspects of the Arts and Crafts credo and his skills as a merchant were formidable. His intentions, however, rose above mere commerce. One of the store's aims had been to refine public taste and aesthetic standards in England. Liberty couture was famous for its light silks printed in softly coloured patterns and was praised by the 1883 exhibition of the Rational Dress Association. Its informal designs made in natural 'art fabrics' were in stark contrast to formal women's dress produced in the fashion houses of Paris, a bastion that was stormed in 1884

when Liberty opened a store in the capital and 'Le Style Liberty' momentarily eclipsed French couture. Liberty supplied virtually everything for the fashionable *fin-de-siècle* aesthete, a pretension that was gently pilloried in the opening of Gilbert and Sullivan's operetta *Patience,* in which languid young ladies were found in precisely the sort of 'aesthetic draperies' bought by fashionable upper middle-class women of finer sensibilities.

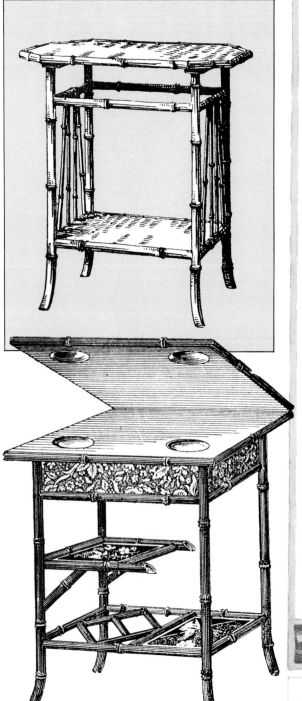

LEFT Small bamboo table covered with 'Old Gold' matting, produced by Liberty and Co.

BELOW LEFT Bamboo card table by Liberty and Co., mounted with gold-leather paper.

RIGHT Silver and
enamel pendant by
Omar Ramsden,
c. 1900.

BELOW RIGHT 'Tudric'
tea set designed for
Liberty and Co. by
Archibald Knox, 1904.

BELOW Worcester teapot in the
form of an Aesthete, inspired by
the operetta Patience.

RIGHT Poster for the operetta
Patience by H.M. Brock.

'THE HIGH AESTHETIC LINE'

Patience provided a good entrée, albeit in satirical form, into the world and the pretensions of the aesthete and the way in which artistic sensibilities were perceived. Distinct from the bourgeois philistine, the 'super aesthetical ultra poetical' men and women who patronized Liberty's store saw art as a consuming passion that absorbed the senses, leaving no room for the mundane realities of life. As one of the operetta's characters observed:

There is a transcendentality in delirium – an acute accentuation of supremest ecstasy – which the earthly might easily mistake for indigestion.

The pretensions pilloried by Gilbert and Sullivan were evident in the literary and artistic figures lionized by fashionable society, notably Wilde and Whistler. Wilde had been educated at Trinity College, Dublin, and had come into contact with Ruskin, Matthew Arnold and Walter Pater at Oxford. In London society his flamboyant dress and manner – later to become an obligatory part of the Aesthete's uniform – attracted instant attention. Wilde's apparel was invariably eccentric consisting of velvet knee breeches and frockcoat, the latter garnished with a lily, which, together with the sunflower and peacock feather became the commonly recognized symbols of aestheticism.

In 1882 Oscar Wilde exported the Aesthetic creed to North America during an 18-month-long lecture tour taking in major cities in both Canada and the United States. The original purpose of the tour, according to Wilde, had been to offer culture to a wealthy, clever but not particularly cultivated nation. Wilde lectured on three basic themes: 'Art and the Handicraftsman', 'Interior Decoration' and the 'English Renaissance in Art'. The content of the lectures was often muddled and indiscriminately linked trends and styles that were quite distinct in origin. The beauty of machinery, Keats, Pre-Raphaelitism, Ruskin, Morris, the stylistic influences of Classical Greece and the Orient were just some of the themes touched upon in his lectures. One has only to consider the difference between two of his themes – 'Morris' and 'machinery' – to catch a glimpse of some of the inconsistencies that riddled his work. Despite these contradictions, Wilde appears to have been a great success in the United States. Several provincial newspapers took umbrage with his foppish and exclusive manner, but the vast majority of his audiences, particularly leisured society women, listened in awe to his pronouncements.

Although Oscar Wilde indiscriminately championed the cause of a variety of progressive but contradicting artistic styles, the Aesthetic cult with which he is associated had a credo of its own. Wilde's aristocratic and elitist posturing was, in fact, party to a well-defined artistic theory and one very different to the theories associated with the Arts and Crafts. The 19th-century French critic and writer Théophile Gautier had argued that art need have no purpose. He had indicated that the pursuit of beauty was a perfectly legitimate end in itself and that art need not be justified by moral or ethical concerns, principles that had hitherto preoccupied art and literature for

THE SIX-MARK TEA-POT.

Æsthetic Bridegroom. "It is quite consummate, is it not?"
Intense Bride. "It is, indeed! Oh, Algernon, let us live up to it!"

centuries. The theory that art could be made or written for its own sake appeared in England and gradually led to a schism between artists, writers and the public at large. Swinburne, writing in 1866, asked ' . . . whether or not the domestic circle is to be for all men and writers the outer limit and extreme horizon of their world of work'. The arena in which some poets and painters were increasingly operating did not require public interest or approval and at times deliberately sought to outrage bourgeois standards of taste and convention. Themes of sexual excess were often addressed by painters such as Beardsley and poets such as Baudelaire, Verlaine, Swinburne and Wilde, demonstrating the triumph of unfettered feeling over convention.

The notion that art need serve no particular purpose was partly developed by Wilde's mentor Walter Pater. Pater had insisted that the appreciation of art or nature was a largely personal issue and had declined to set an absolute standard to which artists or writers might aspire. By current standards Pater's ideas hardly seem remarkable, although it is important to remember that in the mid-19th century such ideas were trying to displace a centuries-old academic tradition that maintained that timeless standards of beauty had been set by Classical antiquity and it was to these that artists and writers should always aspire.

Wilde betrayed a strong influence by Pater and wrote a popular account of Aesthetic conventions in the dialogue between two characters, Ernest and Gilbert, in *The Critic as Artist*, written in 1891. Their discussion showed the new role into which Wilde had cast literature, art and design. The Arts and Crafts tradition had stated that art could not only be taught, but that a germ of creativity could be found in all men and women. It had been beliefs such as these that had led Ruskin to celebrate some of the technical inadequacies of medieval craftsmen and had led C.R. Ashbee to recruit unskilled labour in the Guild and School of Handicraft. In contrast, Wilde promoted a characteristically exclusive view that anything worth knowing could not be taught. In the rarefied atmosphere of the 'artistic' society depicted in Wilde's *The Critic as Artist*, access into the arcane world of art is subject to an aesthetic grace that no amount of training or learning could induce. Art was useless and its qualities needed no explanation or justification. If prosaic souls did not have the sublime wherewithal to appreciate its merits there was little that artist or critic could do. For some late 19th-century painters, critics and poets, the arts were devoid of purpose and became increasingly self-obsessed. Painting became predominantly concerned with superficial form rather than with any story or idea. Poetry became equally self-obsessed, concentrating on metre and rhyme rather than subject matter. Music for this reason was seen as an appropriate Aesthetic medium: it had the unique capacity to touch the senses without any obvious material reference to the mundane everyday world.

Some impression of the insular way in which art was perceived was given by Wilde when he discussed the purpose of criticism. The purpose of the critic is not to act as a mediator between artist and public but rather to record impressions and feelings. Criticism has the capacity to be as sublime, or even more sublime, than the works on which it passes comment. Wilde wrote:

*LEFT Mahogany
cabinet by E.W.
Godwin and J.A.M.
Whistler, exhibited at
the 1878 Exposition
Universelle in Paris.*

RIGHT Illustration of the Tower House and Queen Anne's Grove, Bedford Park, London, by A.N. Grautschold, 1882.

... Who cares whether Mr. Ruskin's views on Turner are sound or not? What does it matter? That mighty and majestic prose of his so fervid and so fiery-coloured in its noble eloquence, so rich in its elaborate symphonic music, so sure and certain, at its best, in subtle choice of word and epithet, is at least as great a work of art as any of those wonderful sunsets that bleach or rot on their corrupted canvasses in England's Gallery ...

The decorative arts assumed particular significance for the Aesthete. Painting, even the avant-garde painting of the Impressionists, was on occasion considered too self-consciously intellectual in that it was a vehicle for ideas of one description or another. The applied or decorative arts, however, had none of the didactic qualities associated with painting, they simply existed in their own state of beauty, more sublime for the simple fact that they had no artistic pretensions whatsoever. They were empty vessels in which the refined spirit of the Aesthete could pour any amount of arcane and refined feeling. Wilde, or more accurately his character Gilbert, explained:

Still, the art that is frankly decorative is the art to live with. It is, of all visible arts, the one art that creates in both mood and temperament. Mere colour, unspoiled by meaning, and unallied with definite form, can speak to the soul in a thousand different ways ...

He continued:

By its deliberate rejection of Nature as the ideal of beauty, as well as of the imitative method of the ordinary painter, decorative art not merely prepares the soul for the reception of true imaginative work, but develops in it that sense of form which is the basis of creative no less than critical achievement.

George Du Maurier passed comment on the sublime qualities of the decorative arts in a *Punch* cartoon. An 'Intense' bride and her 'Aesthetic' groom, surrounded by suitably Aesthetic furniture, inspect a teapot. 'It is quite consummate, is it not?' asks the groom. 'It is indeed!' the bride replies. 'Oh Algernon, let us live up to it!'

Although the 'artistic' fabric and objects from Liberty's store, the pretensions of Wilde and the characters of Du Maurier's cartoons and W.S. Gilbert's libretti were muddled in the popular imagination with the work of the Arts and Crafts Movement, closer inspection shows that they were in fact very different in aims and temperament. The difference between the

Aesthetic tradition and that of the Arts and Crafts Movement was brought sharply into focus in 1877, in a famous dispute between the painter James Abbott McNeill Whistler and John Ruskin.

The dispute centred around the now famous libellous comment made by Ruskin in the July 1877 edition of the *Fors Clavigera* against a painting by Whistler, *Nocturne in Black and Gold*, painted in 1875 and exhibited at the Grosvenor Gallery two years later. With characteristic vitriol Ruskin stated:

For Mr Whistler's own sake, no less than for the protection of the purchaser, Sir Coutts Lindsay ought not to have admitted works into the Gallery in which the ill educated conceit of the artist so nearly approached the aspect of willful imposture. I have seen, and heard, much of cockney impudence before now; but never expected to hear a coxcomb ask two hundred guineas for flinging a pot of paint in the public's face.

Ruskin was too ill to attend court, although several painters inspired by the critic's work were called in his defence, among them Edward Burne-Jones. The cross-examination that followed concerned the degree of 'finish' in Whistler's painting. Burne-Jones expressed appreciation for the colour and atmosphere in *Nocturne,* but was unable to see any composition or detail in the painting to warrant the price asked in the Grosvenor Gallery. Burne-Jones stated to the court that he considered the work little more than a sketch. A painting of

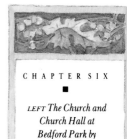

LEFT The Church and Church Hall at Bedford Park by Maurice B. Adams and Richard Norman Shaw.

the Venetian Doge, Andre Gritti, believed to be by Titian, was brought into the court as an example of a work containing the finish Whistler's work so clearly lacked. The painting was, in essence, more overtly naturalistic; in Burne-Jones' words: 'It is a very perfect example of the highest finish of ancient art. The flesh is perfect, the modelling of the face is round and good . . . . [it] is an "arrangement in flesh and blood!"' Similar sentiments were expressed by one W.P. Frith, a Royal Academician, and by Tom Taylor, a contributor to the *Times* and the editor of *Punch*. Both men believed the colour in the painting to be pleasing enough, although neither could see any real attempt on Whistler's part to approach the standards demanded by Ruskin, namely, that painting should reproduce natural appearances. The preoccupation with finish was exacerbated both by the price Whistler demanded for his *Nocturne* and for the time it took him to paint it. Popular opinion maintained that the amount of effort and visible handiwork that went into a picture reflected to a large extent upon its artistic and ultimately its financial worth. Whistler would submit to none of these Ruskinian standards and argued that although the picture took only a day or two to paint it contained the 'knowledge of a lifetime'. The value of the painting, then, was characterized not as craftsmanship, its merit visible in handiwork, but rather as something quite elusive that defies definition.

Whistler's defence of his work makes interesting reading and demonstrates the extent to which the principles of Aestheticism differed from those of Ruskin and the Arts and Crafts Movement. Under cross-examination from Ruskin's counsel, Whistler ambiguously described his *Nocturne in Black and Gold*. It was, he stated, a night piece representing fireworks rather than a simple record of landscape, and, to the mirth of the court, he conceded that if it was called a view it would bring about nothing but disappointment. Whistler tellingly described the painting as an 'artistic arrangement', an abstract term that could apply to a number of his pictures given titles more appropriate to pieces of music than painting. The comparison with music is an interesting one. Although it is possible to demand a precise meaning from pictures – and this was certainly the view taken by Ruskin and his followers – it is harder to make similar demands upon music. Music can be evocative, as indeed can the paintings of Whistler, although it would be difficult to attribute to it any concrete and readily explicable meaning. Whistler had pointed out to Ruskin's overly literal counsel, desperate to read something concrete in his painting, that he could, in fact, impose anything he liked upon the picture. 'My whole scheme', Whistler explained, 'was only to bring about a certain harmony of colour'. Whistler thus emphasized the importance of the form of the picture at the expense of the content, a

BELOW RIGHT
*The main
entrance to the
Glasgow School of Art
by C.R. Mackintosh.
Construction of the
school took place
between 1897 and
1899.*

BELOW FAR RIGHT
*The library
at the Glasgow School
of Art by Charles
Rennie Mackintosh.
Mackintosh's proposal
was the successful entry
in a competition to
design the school held
in 1896.*

preoccupation evident in the ideas of writers associated with Aestheticism and also with some architects connected with the movement.

Whistler's ideas had mystified the court. It is important to recognize that the approbation of the public terrified the Aesthete. Wilde, in the guise of Gilbert, had stated unequivocally in *The Critic as Artist* that he lived in fear of 'not being misunderstood'. Whistler echoed something of this sentiment. He held that none but an artist could be a competent critic of his work, and was not disturbed to discover that his work mystified the general public. His position became even more extreme when he attacked not only the philistine but also the growing number of those who had expressed an interest in things artistic. In the *Ten O'Clock Lecture* of 1885, Whistler completely ridiculed the idea of an empathy between artists and their public. He maintained that artists had always been set apart from the public and that, following the Industrial Revolution, art had been relegated to an object of mere curiosity, becoming little more than a fad and the preserve of a public meddling in something about which they knew little.

Aesthetes, no matter how otherworldly, re-

quired a roof over their heads and Aestheticism extended into architecture and particularly into relatively modest town and suburban housing. In many instances, the architecture associated with the Aesthetic Movement differs little in appearance from that connected with the Arts and Crafts. Both depend heavily upon vernacular styles and traditions of building and consistent attempts are made to reconcile the design of the exterior with that of the interior and its contents. The principal distinction centres, again, upon the motive of architect. In general, the radical calling that inspired Arts and Crafts architecture is absent in that connected with Aestheticism.

One of the first building projects connected with the cult of Aestheticism was the suburban estate at Bedford Park. Jonathan T. Carr had bought the site in the suburbs of west London in 1875 and began to develop an entire village designed to appeal to an artistically aware middle-class clientele keen to leave the city for an idealized version of a small rural community. The project began in 1877 and included not only homes but also schools, an inn, a clubhouse, a church and an art school. A number of architects were contracted to work

on the project. E.W. Godwin was involved in the early stages of the development, although Bedford Park is principally associated with Richard Norman Shaw. The appearance of the houses – which William Morris disliked intensely – tends to differ, although most are variations on the 'Queen Anne' style that was to have such a resonant appeal in the United States. The houses were mostly constructed in red brick and often had hanging tiles, steeply pitched and gabled roofs, and leaded windows; they were fronted by gardens with sunflowers, the statutory symbol of Aestheticism. The style is only loosely associated with Queen Anne and the early 18th century. The buildings are, in fact, a blend of several styles and were generally intended to give the impression of an old English village rather than to reconstruct a community with any great architectural accuracy. Robert McLeod, in his study of recent English architecture, observed that the design of the houses is predominantly inspired by a concern for formal appearance and overall visual effect rather than practical utility. Many of the buildings show a marked feel for balancing architectural forms and motifs with less regard for the living conditions within. This interest in abstraction of form, colour and metre also occurred in the art and poetry associated with Aestheticism.

Bedford Park attracted a variety of middle-class residents, many of whom were in some sense artistically inclined or of radical sympathies. They included artists, actors, writers and architects. Voysey lived there for a short period, as did the Irish Nationalist John O'Leary. Membership of 'a high aesthetic band' was by no means obligatory. Bedford Park sustained enough families to supply a conventional church-school, different in persuasion to the more liberal, co-educational alternative preferred by the more radical residents. In the popular imagination, however, Bedford Park became inextricably associated with the pretensions of Aestheticism.

The 'elite' of Aestheticism were found not in the genteel avenues of Bedford Park but in Chelsea. Among the residents around Tite Street were Whistler, Sargent, Sickert, Wilde, his friend Frank Miles, and Carlo Pelligrini, together with a substantial band of now largely forgotten acolytes. E.W. Godwin designed a number of homes and studios in the district.

He had initially worked in the Gothic and Queen Anne styles, although he abandoned, or attempted to abandon, these in favour of a more aggressively formal style of building that anticipates the appearance of much 20th-century architecture. His designs for the White House, Whistler's studio, shed the surface decoration of Queen Anne and juxtaposed large areas of undecorated stuccoed wall and roof space, interrupted only by the inclusion of simple unadorned windows. The Metropolitan Board of Works so disliked the stark simplicity of the building that it insisted that some decoration in the form of relief sculpture be added to the exterior. Some compromises were made, although the sculptures were never included on the façade. The Board took even greater exception to another of Godwin's buildings, designed for Frank Miles at number 44 Tite Street. Again, the house was originally to be composed of interlocking geometric forms with virtually no surface decoration. The Board insisted that a Flemish-style gable be added and the balcony be altered to soften the aggressive appearance of the exterior.

ABOVE Design for a living room by M.H. Baillie-Scott, 1911.

A tendency toward novelty, and formal simplicity, was to become an increasingly important feature in the evolution of European architecture and design. Designers such as C.F.A. Voysey and Charles Rennie Mackintosh evolved a style of building that primarily exploited the creative possibilities of often stark architectural form. In addition, there was a tendency to abandon the example of history as a source of inspiration in building and develop new architectural forms and motifs. Mackay Hugh Baillie-Scott evolved a very individual style. His buildings followed the example of architects and designers of the Arts and Crafts Movement in that the interior and exterior are co-ordinated as one total design, yet his fanciful style is light years away from the practical designs of, say, Gimson or Stickley. Architecture, for Baillie-Scott, rather appeared as a 'charmed territory' in which to pursue adventures in colour, form and space with little regard for history or convention. The decorated organic designs for the interior and the furniture made in 1898 for the Grand Duke of Hesse at the Palace at Darmstadt give a clear insight into his latent romanticism. Simplicity and the absence of historical precedent are marked most notably in the works of the Glasgow Four, C.R. Mackintosh, Herbert MacNair, and Frances and Margaret MacDonald. Some examples of their work admit the odd historical detail. Mackintosh's School of Art at Glasgow grudgingly includes some Tudor motifs, although much of his work is very simple in design and decorated only with organic and geometric motifs devoid of any historical association. Hill House in Helensburgh, Scotland, is an excellent example of Mackintosh's formal purity.

This concern with form and with the pursuit of abstract and often obscure artistic ideals preoccupied many artists and designers in the early 20th century throughout Europe and the United States. The democratic ideal of the Arts and Crafts Movement, the notion that art could serve a purpose and be used as an object of social utility was, however, to be taken up again. In 20th-century Europe the most intelligent reading of the craft ideal occurs not specifically in England, but in Austria and particularly in Germany, with the foundation of the Deutscher Werkbund and the Weimar Bauhaus.

■

LEFT Hill House at Helensburgh, Scotland, by C.R. Mackintosh. The house was designed for the publisher William Blackie in 1900.

CHAPTER SEVEN

THE EUROPEAN CONTRIBUTION

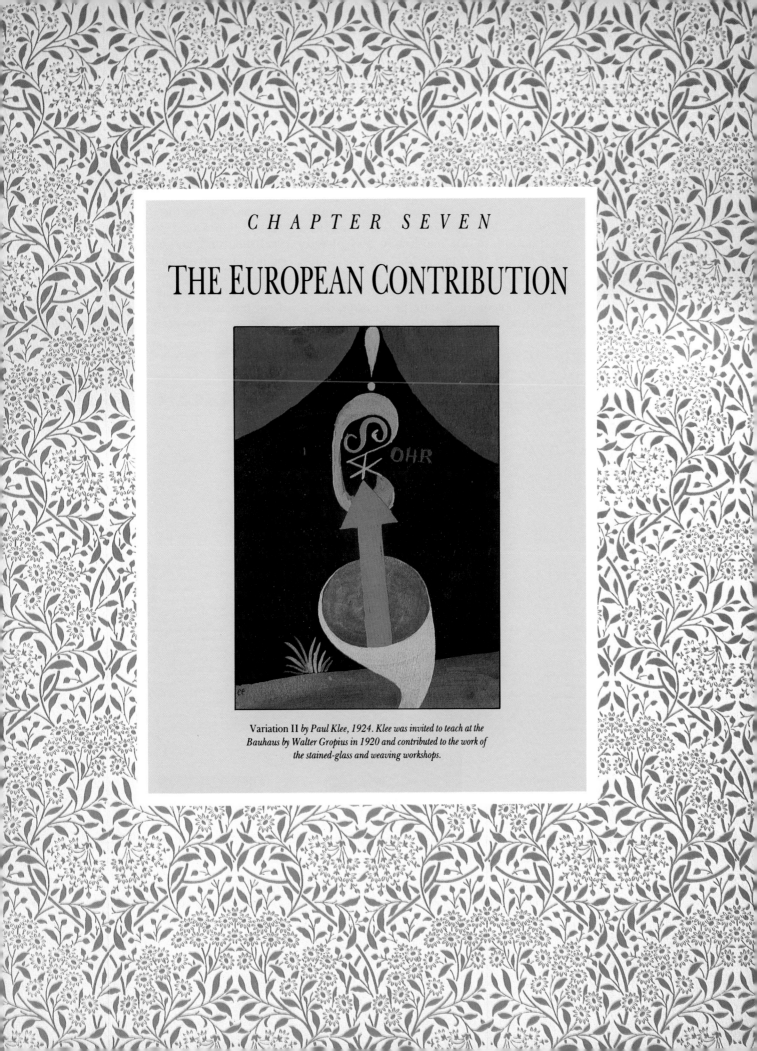

Variation II by Paul Klee, 1924. Klee was invited to teach at the
Bauhaus by Walter Gropius in 1920 and contributed to the work of
the stained-glass and weaving workshops.

Charles Robert Ashbee had said that the principles of the Arts and Crafts Movement were more consistently and logically developed in the United States and Europe than in Britain. The consistency of the American contribution to the movement has already been shown in some detail: architects and designers such as Gustav Stickley, Greene and Greene and Frank Lloyd Wright took on many of the problems of design, production, distribution and consumption that had haunted the

Arts and Crafts Movement since its inception. With the assistance of machinery they were able to make significant amendments to the Arts and Crafts tradition and nurse the movement away from the well-intentioned but ultimately impractical phase of Utopian socialist craftsmanship, and some way toward the long-standing goal of making well-designed and good quality furniture for larger and less exclusive markets than those for which most British designers had worked.

A sense of consistency and logic is found not

only in the work of American artists and craftsmen but also in that of many European designers, notably those working in Germany during the first decades of this century. Not all British craftsmen and women, however, were adherents to a tradition preoccupied only with the pernicious effects of industrialism and a lost medieval ideal of handicrafts and labour. The architect William Richard Lethaby (1857-1931) had attempted to help design and industry coexist and had considered establishing an association, similar to the Werkbund in Germany, that would foster links between what, in English circles, had traditionally been regarded as bitter opponents.

Lethaby provided an interesting staging post between the romantic but impractical stage within the evolution of the Arts and Crafts Movement and the realistic integration of art and industry that was to occur with the Werkstätte, Werkbund and Bauhaus in Austria and Germany. Lethaby was born in Barnstaple in 1857 and was originally apprenticed to a local architect concerned primarily

LEFT Brockhampton Church (All Saints) in Herefordshire by William Richard Lethaby, 1901.

■

RIGHT Doors of the Willow Tea Rooms, Glasgow, by C.R. Mackintosh, 1904.

with the construction of practical farm buildings. At the age of 22 he became the chief clerk in Richard Norman Shaw's practice and worked intermittently for Morris and with Kenton and Co. At first glance Lethaby's ideas on art and architecture appear to be contradictory. On the one hand, he was acutely conscious of architectural tradition; he admired medieval building and was active within the Society for the Protection of Ancient Buildings. On the other hand he appeared to advocate something approaching a functionalist aesthetic. Lethaby constantly stressed the importance of efficiency of purpose, describing art as the 'well doing of what needs doing'. He was suspicious of artistic considerations in architecture and matters of taste. 'I would', he wrote, 'have buildings tested by such generally understandable ideas as fitness, soundness, economy, efficiency, reasonableness, intelligibility, carefulness, science and mastery . . . . There are two dozen words of this type which I should like to become the stock in trade of architectural critics.' Lethaby, in addition, was involved with the Design and Industries Association, a cooperative venture between artists, designers, producers, teachers and consumers that admitted the importance of mechanized industry to modern design.

The key that enables one to reconcile Lethaby's simultaneous admiration for both the architectural conventions of the past and the innovations of the present was his appreciation of the place of building within history. Building, for Lethaby, was an organic part of the cultural environment from which it sprang and, at its best, represented a tradition that need not be thought of in self-consciously artistic terms. It is interesting to note that Morris had spoken of medieval art in a similar context, finding within it an 'unconscious intelligence'.

For Lethaby, architecture need not be isolated and considered as some specialist refined realm of sensibility. A more healthy alternative, and one that Lethaby believed to have existed in the Middle Ages, was an environment where individual creativity was a commonplace human attribute, and sound building evolved out of spiritual and practical necessity of the period. Consequently, a medieval church, say, was built and decorated from local material with local skill, to fulfil an estab-

lished spiritual need. The same basic principle could be applied to any era. The appearance of building would necessarily change as needs within the community changed. However, the traditions of building and of practicality remained the same. It was this tradition of sound, practical and purposeful construction that, as far as architecture was concerned, historically linked the past with the present. Change should be written into sound architecture and design, and in this sense Lethaby was distinctly modern in his approach.

In his writing, however, Lethaby introduced a caveat to explain the process by which change should occur: sound building, he believed, should concentrate on the modification of traditional forms. His church at Brockhampton-by-Ross, in Herefordshire, is an impressive practical example of his approach. The simply designed church is constructed with massive piers made partly with coke-breeze concrete on a stone string course. The modern concrete, however, supports oak purlins which themselves carry a traditional thatched roof. Speaking of the way in which modern requirements are grafted on to tradition, Lethaby had stated that a well-designed 'table or chair or book has to be very well bred.' In this sense, then, Lethaby was dependent upon an historical tradition but unlike some members of the Arts and Crafts Movement he did not connect tradition with any particular style. History, for Lethaby, found form in a tradition of common-sense practicality that spanned the centuries.

Lethaby applied this blend of respect for the past and the practical recognition of the needs and demands of the present at the Central School of Art where, together with George Frampton, he was appointed co-principal. Halsey Ricardo, who taught architecture under Lethaby at the Central School, advised students that his classes were concerned with practical issues rather than style, and it was from this practicality, Ricardo stated, that beauty sprang. The school's programme focused primarily on the applied arts and actively sought to serve the needs of industry. The fine arts were only admitted into the curriculum as adjuncts to the more practical and useful disciplines.

The school's prime concerns fell in the categories of metalwork, the production of books,

CHAPTER SEVEN

RIGHT The Sezession Building, Vienna, by Joseph Maria Olbrich, 1897–98.

building, decoration, woodwork and cabinet-making, and carving. The bulk of the school's activities was concentrated in the evening, enabling both students and teachers to participate in industry. Unlike their contemporaries in more academic schools, they would, either as students or designers, have the practical day-to-day experience that was absent in more conventional art education.

Despite Lethaby's importance in the evolution of the Arts and Crafts Movement, the nettle of industrialism was grasped with far greater confidence not in England but in centres throughout Europe, particularly in German-speaking countries.

The Arts and Crafts had first been exported to Europe through a number of channels. The work of Ashbee and Baillie-Scott at Darmstadt attracted great attention in Germany and had a direct influence on the works of both German and Austrian architects. The work of the Guild and School of Handicraft was represented at exhibitions in Berlin and Vienna together with submissions from French, Belgian and Scottish designers. C.R. Mackintosh's aggressively modern designs were ecstatically received by Viennese architects who were labouring under the weight of parochial interpretations of bastardized classical and Gothic traditions. *The Studio*, a progressive magazine with accounts of the fine and applied arts from a number of European centres, was another important means of disseminating ideas.

Interest in the British Arts and Crafts Movement was not only limited to aesthetic concerns. Germany was rapidly emerging as a powerful industrial nation and was eager to learn from the example of British designers and architects. In fact, Hermann Muthesius, an attaché to the German Embassy in Britain, was despatched in 1896 to provide an account of British prowess in the fields of architecture and design. (He wrote the seminal study *Das Englische Haus* from his research.)

At the beginning of the century, progressive styles in British design and architecture were absorbed with little distinction between the often different attitudes of the architects concerned. In centres such as Vienna, modernity often appeared to have been far more important than the formation of a theoretically sound aesthetic doctrine. This interest in progressive styles devoid of an historical association was caused by a reaction toward a long tradition of support for conventional art and architecture based upon the constant repetition of past styles.

The Secession group, established in Vienna in 1897 by a number of avant-garde artists who had seceded from the conservative *Künstlerhaus*, had no hard and fast aesthetic party line. Its prime concern was that those in its ranks should avoid the oppressive example of history and begin to create anew; as the movement's declamatory maxim stated, 'To the Age its Art, to Art its Freedom'.

The Secession distinguished itself from the more conventional *Künstlerhaus* by a general desire to promote modern art, to avoid the trappings of commerce in art and to establish a direct relationship with the public. The movement also insisted that there should be no traditional division between the applied and fine arts, believing both to be of equal worth. The Secession's eighth exhibition (primarily of applied rather than fine arts) contained submissions from a number of avant-garde artists and designers throughout Europe who, in the main, had also attempted to reject the past and forge a novel and often radically simple style. Among the exhibits were the works of the French Maison Moderne and of the Belgian designer Henri Van de Velde. Ashbee was also represented, although it is doubtful whether the ideals of the Guild and School of Handicraft were fully appreciated by the Secession.

Of far more immediate interest to the Secessionist was the ascetic, geometric but still ultimately decorative style of Charles Rennie Mackintosh. Like the florid, organic Art Nouveau style that had blossomed in France, the Secession style also rejected the past and based its forms upon ahistorical motifs, but instead of employing forms from nature, it took geometry as its principal starting point. This decorative use of geometry, as distinct from the functional application it was given by contemporary architects such as Adolf Loos (1870–1933), is evident in much of the work of the Secession. It occurs in Joseph Maria Olbrich's (1867–1908) Secession building and appears in his designs for metalwork and in the glass designed by his contemporary Koloman Moser (1868–1918). In each case geometry is used as an aesthetic source rather than as an entrée into a rational design.

WIENER WERKSTÄTTE

Many members of the Secession were also active in the Wiener Werkstätte. Founded in 1903 by Josef Hoffmann and Koloman Moser and financed by Fritz Waerndorfer and Otto Primavesi, the Werkstätte were influenced by the example of Ashbee in England and the many craft workshops that were springing up in Germany, and also claimed kinship with Ruskin and Morris. In their Werkstätte manifesto, Hoffmann and Moser made no distinction between the fine and applied arts, and stressed that the design of objects should reflect the innate qualities of the materials from which they were made. These principles were applied to virtually all conceivable fields, from architecture and interior design to fashion and cutlery, all of which were to be coordinated to reflect a distinctly modern spirit. The Werkstätte maintained a very high public profile in both national and international exhibitions in Vienna, Rome, Cologne and Paris, and stores selling Werkstätte products were located not only in fashionable quarters of Vienna but also in Germany, Switzerland and the United States.

The Wiener Werkstätte, as Jane Kallir has noted, were ambivalent in their attitude toward industry, vacillating between a respect for the hand-crafted and the realization that no contemporary design workshop could ignore the increasing trend toward industrialization. A high respect for craftsmanship and the creative autonomy of its designers, a strong antipathy toward poorly designed and mass-produced goods, and funding from wealthy patrons did nothing to help the Werkstätte face up to the harsher side of the business world. In practice, the workshops' ideals proved contradictory. They wanted to produce 'good and simple articles for everyday use' but, following the example of Ruskin and Morris, were not prepared to compromise the working conditions of their craftsmen to achieve this end. They stated:

We cannot and will not compete with cheap work, which has succeeded largely at the expense of the worker. We have made it our foremost duty to help the worker recover pleasure in his task and

OPPOSITE, FAR LEFT *Inkwell produced by the Wiener Werkstätte*

OPPOSITE RIGHT *Reclining chair by Josef Hoffmann, c. 1905.*

ABOVE LEFT *Vase with glass liner by Hoffmann, c. 1905.*

ABOVE RIGHT *Oak table by Hoffmann, c. 1903.*

BELOW *Tea service by the Wiener Werkstätte.*

obtain humane conditions in which to carry it out . . .

These were noble and costly ideals and throughout their history the Wiener Werkstätte were financed to a dangerously high degree by advances from patrons or friends to complete projects, after which their funds would be desperately depleted. Kallir, in her study *Viennese Design and the Wiener Werkstätte*, noted the chronic financial problems faced by the Werkstätte which nonetheless miraculously lasted for well over two decades until their final demise in 1932.

The Wiener Werkstätte never resolved the conflict between their admiration for the time-honoured principles of craftsmanship and their recognition of the inevitability of mechanized production. The Viennese architect and contemporary of Hoffmann, Adolf Loos, however, began to embrace the prospect of a purpose-built, machine-produced environment with greater confidence. Loos did not believe that architecture or design should be made to appear modern for its own sake, and in an essay written in 1908 he criticized some craft workshops for being self-consciously contemporary, for thrusting a 'podgy hand in the spinning wheel of time'. Loos' attitude to the historical development of design is similar to that of Lethaby. He wrote:

No man – nor any association – had to create our wardrobes, our cigarette boxes, our jewellery. Time created them for us. They change from year to year, from day to day, from hour to hour. For we ourselves change from hour to hour and with us our attitudes and habits. This is how our culture has changed . . . . We do not sit in a particular way because a carpenter has made a chair in such and such a manner. A carpenter makes a chair in a particular manner because that is how we wish to sit.

Loos advocated that the design of something should be determined by its function and in his essay on the historical pretensions of Viennese architecture, 'Potemkin's Town', he criticized Viennese architecture for its patently unrealistic aspirations. A series of apartments occupied by people of limited means should, he felt, be represented as modest dwellings rather than dressed in some wholly inappropriate Gothic or classical garb. There was no shame, he believed, in using inexpensive materials to build homes for ordinary people. Of greatest importance was the quality of the craftsmanship and, above all, honest design.

The idea that the appearance could be fashioned by utility was also taken up by Hermann Muthesius in *Das Englische Haus*. Muthesius was particularly taken with the humble bourgeois character of English building. The cultural identity of the middle classes in Germany was poorly established and bourgeois culture was often nothing other than a pale imitation of the culture of the aristocracy. In England, however, the middle classes had been long established as a cultural force, they had a clear cultural identity and

demonstrated a strong sense of practicality, independence and self-confidence in their style of living. Muthesius particularly admired the self-effacing style of British vernacular building and felt that its simple character was symptomatic of the way in which the British bourgeoisie felt no need to imitate the manners of their social superiors. Such buildings, he felt, evolved out of practical necessity; windows in English homes, for example, were placed where they were needed and not simply to satisfy the demands of architectural unity. The prime concern for the Englishman's home was comfort. Muthesius listed the 'Exemplary qualities in the English House'.

English houses, as we can see, are wisely reduced to essentials and adapted to given circumstances; the point, therefore, that is worth copying from them is the emphasis that is laid on purely objective requirements. The Englishman builds his house for himself alone. He feels no urge to impress, has no thought of festive occasions or banquets and the idea of shining in the eyes of the world through lavishness in and of his house simply does not occur to him. Indeed, he even avoids attracting attention to his house by means of striking design or architectonic extravagance, just as he would be loth to appear personally eccentric by wearing a fantastic

FAR LEFT Annesley Lodge, Platts Lane, Hampstead, London, by C.F.A. Voysey, 1895.

LEFT The Tristan Tzara House, Paris, by Adolf Loos, 1926–27.

suit. In particular, the architectonic ostentation, the creation of 'architecture' and 'style' to which we in Germany are still so prone, is no longer to be found in England.

Muthesius exerted a strong influence on the German cultural establishment and in 1907 he was appointed to the Chair of Applied Arts in the Berlin Trade School. His polemical address to the school gave a damning account of the backward-looking attitudes of some contemporary German designers. So damning was the address that it led to a schism. Two factions were to emerge within the school. The first was reactionary and petitioned the Kaiser for Muthesius' resignation. This faction had a strong sentimental attachment to the German ideal of the pre-industrial craft guild, and the same ideal was later to have a strong appeal to the romantic nationalism of the National Socialists. The other faction defended the progressive ideals of Muthesius and were eventually to form part of the Deutscher Werkbund.

The Deutscher Werkbund, a confraternity of craftsmen, architects and industrialists, was formed in 1907 from a number of Werkstätte dedicated to the reform of the applied arts. Newly industrialized Germany had suffered a fate not dissimilar to that of mid-19th-century England. Mass-production had generally compromised the traditional standards of German craftsmanship and the Werkbund was seen as a society for reform. Yet it is important to state from the outset that 'reform' meant different things to different craftsmen. The Werkbund contained a broad spectrum of opinion, one significant strand of which centred very strongly upon Muthesius' influence and the reform of design with the aid of mechanized industry. Such reforms had already begun, or at least been considered, by the Dresden Werkstätte, one of the most influential within the Werkbund. Established in 1898 according to Ruskinian principles of un-alienated labour and creative fulfilment, its founder Karl Schmidt was nonetheless quite able to reconcile his concern for the well-being of his workforce to the use of machinery and even to standardized techniques of production. It is worth noting that mass-production was criticized in Germany, yet many designers and architects were able to see that in the right hands machinery could be re-directed to produce well-designed goods. British designers, by contrast, were on the whole more timorous and most, at best, only grudgingly compromised with machinery. Other workshops,

*RIGHT The dining
room of the Haus
Freudenberg by
Hermann Muthesius,
1912.*

craftsmen and industrialists rallied to Muthesius' cause, among them the Austrians Hoffmann and Olbrich. Peter Behrens, who was attached to the electrical manufacturers AEG as a resident designer and architect, was also active in its foundation of the Werkbund, as were Bruno Paul, Richard Riemerschmid and Theodor Fischer. Industrialists in the field of glass manufacture, metalwork, weaving and publishing were also represented, motivated, in part, by the hope that a coalition between workers and benign industrialists might serve as an antidote to socialism and workers' control of industry.

The Werkbund, through the medium of an ever-growing number of provincial offices, hoped to establish a clear and unified direction for German art and industry. Sound design was applied not only to domestic goods but also to heavy industry. Conspicuously well-designed goods would, it was hoped, establish an unmistakably German identity in product design and increase its international standing among trade competitors. Naumann believed that Germany's economic health and reputation should be founded not on direct competition with its industrialized neighbours but on the development of expertise in specialized fields. Muthesius played upon such nationalistic tendencies by associating the patronage of Werkbund workshops and industries with a German sense of patriotism. The Werkbund undertook a programme to educate public

taste and attempts were made to wean consumers away from the twin evils of traditionalism and novelty. The evangelism of the Werkbund even spread abroad through displays of German design in various diplomatic missions. It is interesting to note that the Werkbund had emerged through the intervention of Muthesius from the Arts and Crafts tradition in England. The redemptive capacity of the English craft ideal was associated not with workers' emancipation and socialism but, in this instance, with the ambitions for German Nationhood. This was eventually to end in war and a significant adjustment of the craft ideal in Germany.

The Werkbund went from strength to strength with almost 2,000 members by the beginning of 1914. Its progress was, however, interrupted by the outbreak of the First World War. It was also distracted by an acrimonious debate between two factions at its exhibition held only months before the eruption of hostilities. Those factions were represented by Muthesius on the one hand and Henri Van de Velde on the other, and the point of conflict centred around the degree of autonomy that should be afforded to the architect or designer. Muthesius had held that design should be standardized to accommodate mass-production and aspired to an almost transcendental logic, wherein the rational spirit of the age rose above the individual creative whim of the designer. Van de Velde, in contrast, upheld in-

dividualism and the creative autonomy of the designer. Prominent members of the Werkbund gravitated toward the two respective causes, although four years later the defeat of Germany had cast mechanization and mass-production in a less than favourable light: machines produced not only domestic goods but weapons in quantity and to disastrous effect. Walter Gropius, who had supported Van de Velde at the Werkbund and, incidentally, saw active service at the front, held that the uncritical admiration of machinery and technological progress was the source of Germany's undoing. It is perhaps significant that the early days of the Weimar Bauhaus were characterized by a marked return to an interest in handicrafts.

The Bauhaus served as one of the last significant staging posts of the Arts and Crafts tradition. It was established in 1919 under the direction of Walter Gropius (1883–1969) and had emerged from the amalgamated schools of fine and applied arts in Weimar with the proposed addition of a new school of architecture. The programme of the Bauhaus contained a number of ideals common to the Arts and Crafts tradition: Gropius had stated that the school aimed to reconcile the fine and applied arts, and to put them to the service of building. The prime point of departure for the Bauhaus curriculum was handicraft. Gropius maintained that there was no real difference between the work of the artist and that of the craftsman and that craft was the proper basis for all creative achievement. Teachers at the Bauhaus were classified as Masters of Form, and craftsmen as Technical Masters. The old academic and class distinctions between the fine and the applied arts, in principle at least, were forgotten. The guild ideal was extended in the relationship between staff and students. Teachers were known as 'masters' and students either as 'apprentices' or 'journeymen'. The curriculum was to consist of an initial six-month preliminary course, after which students would receive training under the direction of both Masters of Form and Technical Masters. Masters of Form taught theoretical issues under the categories of Observation, Representation and Composition, each of which had their own sub-divisions; and Technical Masters supervised teaching in craft workshops in the fields of stone, wood, metal,

ABOVE LEFT The Allgemeine Elektricitäts Gesellschaft factory before its redesign.

LEFT The redesigned AEG factory by Peter Behrens, 1907–1908.

BELOW LEFT Electric kettle for AEG designed by Behrens, c. 1908.

clay, glass, colour and textiles. The Bauhaus was ill-equipped and was distracted not only by the explosive political climate in post-war Germany but also by internal dissent among members of staff from the old Academy of Fine Arts who were resentful of the Bauhaus' radical new programme. The school was also dogged by half-hearted support from the Weimar authorities and was eventually forced to leave the city for the politically more clement climate of Dessau.

The move to Dessau marked a period of re-organization that served to give the Bauhaus something of the unity of direction it had lacked in Weimar. The aims of the Dessau Bauhaus, as Gillian Naylor has observed, shifted from craft-based activities to the construction of industrial prototypes. The metal-work of Wilhelm Wagenfeld and tubular-steel furniture of Marcel Breuer are notable examples of this shift toward industrial concerns. Gropius also became increasingly interested in standardized design, thus echoing sentiments that had been presented by Muthesius a decade or so earlier. Among the first projects at Dessau was the building of the school itself, consisting of workshops, administrative buildings and accommodation for both staff and students in a style that was at once practical and studiedly contemporary. An estate consisting of inexpensive workers' housing was also undertaken in Dessau and it was around this period that the school became increasing interested in social and statistical theory as the logical point of departure for

architecture and design. The estate consisted of over 300 dwellings assembled from pre-fabricated materials and was to form an ideal modern housing community. Some contemporary observers, however, thought the houses thoroughly 'un-German'.

The Bauhaus was against academic convention and the divisions that traditionally separated art and craft, yet it never followed a one-party line alone. Gropius had championed Van de Velde in the dispute with Muthesius on the creative autonomy of the architect and designer and continued to allow students similar freedoms. Even at Dessau it becomes difficult to pin the school down to anything other than a number of articles of faith focusing on machine production, rational design and an awareness of living in a modern age. Marcel Breuer's much imitated tubular-steel pieces of furniture were not simply rational designs in a new material hitherto reserved for industry. Breuer spoke enigmatically about constructing furniture in space. A functionalist spirit is evident in much of the output from the Bauhaus, yet such abstract interest in artistic form often lurks nearby. Some members of the Bauhaus recognized a contradiction between the respective aims of art and functionalism and realized that what works well need not necessarily look artistic and vice versa. Intellectual consistency was imposed upon the school under the directorship of the left-wing architect Hannes Meyer.

Meyer was appointed as Gropius' successor in 1928 and attempted to inject undiluted

fghi
ppqr
uxyz

social utility into the Bauhaus curriculum, purging many of the distracting 'incestuous' artistic theories that had circulated in the school since its inception. Practical architecture became the dominant interest and theoretical studies revolved around town planning, economics and sociology, with the inclusion of classes in physical exercise as a counter balance to mental labour. Under Meyer's directorship the school even supported its own communist cell. Left-wing ideals found form in the emphasis given to the production of cheap, mass-produced items, to mass-housing programmes and to collective rather than individual work on the part of students. Meyer was ousted from the Bauhaus when his contract was terminated in 1930. His high left-wing political profile was impractical in a political milieu that was steadily lurching to the right. Meyer's career at the Bauhaus marked the effective demise of the Arts and Crafts Movement. The link between Meyer and Morris is a tenuous one, yet aspects of Morris's work – his socialist convictions and his interest in a commonplace, logical, democratic art, often undertaken collectively rather than individually and serving the needs of the common man or woman found more than a passing similarity to the last days of the Bauhaus.

The final days of the school under the direction of Mies van der Rohe are depressing. Attacked by both the left and right wings and fraught with internal unrest, the Bauhaus eventually closed under pressure from the National Socialists in August 1933.

ABOVE LEFT Tea service in silver with wooden handles by Christian Deli, produced at the Bauhaus metal workshop, c. 1925.

LEFT Bauhaus building at Dessau, 1925–26 (from an aerial photograph of 1926).

BELOW LEFT Tubular metal chair. The prototypes for tubular furniture had been produced at the Bauhaus by Marcel Breuer about 1926–27. Chairs closely resembling Breuer's original designs are still in production today.

POSTSCRIPT

Reactionary, revolutionary, romantic and rationalist are, then, epithets applicable to the work of craftsmen and women on both sides of the Atlantic. A survey of the Arts and Crafts Movement, from its origins in the writings of Pugin, Carlyle and Ruskin to its effective demise in Nazi Germany, shows that it is nothing if not diverse. If the Arts and Crafts Movement is so diverse a conglomeration of both theory and practice, what, then, binds it together as a movement?

In order to appreciate the factors that bind Ruskin, Wright, Hubbard, Gropius, Morris and others and to grasp the long-term significance of the Arts and Crafts, one has first to take into account the aims and intentions of other movements in art over the past century or so.

Around the middle of the 19th century, an attitude evolved which maintained that art existed in a vacuum with no direct reference to the society from which it sprang. Art had no particular social use and those that produced it shunned public approval and, in some instances, deliberately courted public censure. This tendency was evident in the art and literature of 19th-century France. It was also apparent in the works of Wilde, Swinburne, and Whistler, as well as the aspirations of Art Nouveau, and it continued in a variety of forms throughout the 20th century. The tradition continues in our own times, in that perfectly ordinary intelligent people are quite unable to understand the art produced by their own society.

The notion that art is a highly refined activity with no particular role; that it has its own arcane, internal logic outside the grasp of the ordinary citizen, and that it is practised by specialists for specialists was vehemently rejected by many within the Arts and Crafts Movement. The movement, albeit in a number of ways, sought to afford art social utility. Under the protection of Pugin, art's purpose was to revive the architectural idiom of the Middle Ages and with it the finer spiritual feelings of the period. For Morris, art was predicated upon fulfiling work – and fulfiling work ultimately demanded vast social and economic change. In addition, art could be purged of much of its sophistication and refinement. For Morris and Ruskin, art became the democratic cultural expression of a community and needed no high priests in the form of artists to exercise the rite. In the United States, the Arts and Crafts tradition was an aid to establish a national identity founded upon independence, work and democracy. In Germany, the Arts and Crafts ideal again has a social application be it (in Muthesius' case) to fashion

a cultural and economic identity for bourgeois Germany or (in the case of the Bauhaus) to propagate, with the aid of machinery, logically designed, mass-produced goods for mass markets.

Public utility and a missionary zeal to improve the lot of producer and consumer are the only call to which all craftsmen and women associated with the Arts and Crafts Movement can easily rally. The call is, however, quite distinct from others to which artists have rallied: unlike the plethora of styles and "isms" that appear throughout the 19th and 20th centuries, the Arts and Crafts, like the arts of the Middle Ages, are projected once again into a public rather than private arena.

The real nature of the Arts and Crafts Movement is one of social purpose rather than style. This is worth remembering in an age when the outward signs of the movement – its picturesque qualities, its taste for a pastoral idyll and the hand-crafted – have made the movement very popular again. The Arts and Crafts Movement finds its true spirit repeated not in Post-Modernist building in homely brick rather than aggressive concrete, or in the pastoral reminiscences of long-dead Edwardian amateurs, or in the romanticism of fashion houses or advertising agencies that trade in resonant ideals of a picturesque countryside, but in the political, social and cultural bulwarks against the age of Gradgrind, an age that is by no means limited to either the 19th century or to England.

OPPOSITE LEFT Arts and Crafts table, casket and candlestick.

OPPOSITE, ABOVE LEFT Hill House, Helensburgh, Scotland, by C.R. Mackintosh.

OPPOSITE, BELOW RIGHT The Haus Freudenberg by Hermann Muthesius, 1912.

BELOW LEFT La Margarete wallpaper panel by Walter Crane.

BELOW Electric fans designed for AEG by Peter Behrens, c. 1908.

ARTS & CRAFTS
■

BIBLIOGRAPHY

The author wishes to acknowledge his debt to many sources and recommends the following select bibliography for further reading:—

ADBURGHAM, Alison, *Liberty's: A Biography of a Shop*, London, 1975.
ANSCOMBE, Isabelle and GERE, Charlotte, *Arts and Crafts in Britain and America*, New York, 1983.
ASLIN, Elizabeth, *The Aesthetic Movement, Prelude to Art Nouveau*, London, 1969.
BENTON, Tim and Charlotte & SHARPE, Denis, (eds.), *Form and Function*, London, 1975.
BROOKS, H. A., *The Prairie School; Frank Lloyd Wright and his Midwest Contemporaries*, Toronto, 1972.
CARLYLE, Thomas, *Past and Present*, London, 1843.
CATLEUGH, Jon, *William De Morgan: Tiles*, London, 1983.
CENTURY GUILD, *The Hobby Horse*, London, 1884–1894.
CLARK, Robert Judson (*et al*), *The Arts and Crafts Movement in America 1876–1916*, Princeton, 1972.
COBDEN-SANDERSON, T., *The Arts and Crafts Movement*, London, 1905.
COMINO, Mary, *Gimson and the Barnsleys*, London, 1980.
CRANE, W., *William Morris to Whistler*, London, 1911.
CRAWFORD, Alan, *C. R. Ashbee: Architect, Designer and Romantic Socialist*, Princeton, 1985.
DOWNING, A. J., *Cottage Residences, or a Series of Designs for Rural Cottages, etc.*, New York, 1842.
ENGELS, Frederich, *Condition of the Working Class in England in 1884*, London, 1984.
EVANS, Joan, *John Ruskin*, London, 1954.
FERBER, Linda S. and GERDTS, W. H. *The New Path: Ruskin and the American Pre-Raphaelites;* New York, 1985.
GIROUARD, Mark, *Sweetness and Light: 'Queen Anne' Movement, 1860–1900*, London, 1984.
GROPIUS, W., *The New Architecture and the Bauhaus*, London, 1935.
HARVIE, Christopher (*et al*), (ed.), *Industrialization and Culture 1830–1914*, London, 1970.
HUBBARD, E., *The Roycroft Shop: A History*, East Aurora, 1909.
JOHNSON, D. C., *American Art Nouveau*, New York, 1979.
KALLIR, Jane, *Viennese Design and The Wiener Werkstätte*, London, 1986.
KLINGENDER, Francis D., *Art and the Industrial Revolution*, London, 1972.
KOCH, Robert, *Louis C. Tiffany, Rebel in Glass*, New York, 1982.
LAMBOURNE, Lionel, *Utopian Craftsmen – The Arts and Crafts Movement from the Cotswolds to Chicago*, London, 1980.
LUCIE SMITH, Edward, *The Story of Craft: the Craftsman's Role in Society*, Oxford, 1981.
LYNES, Russell, *The Tastemakers: The Shaping of American Popular Taste*, New York, 1981.
MCLEOD, Robert, *Style and Society, Architectural Ideology in Britain 1835–1914*, London, 1970.
MORRIS, William, *News From Nowhere*, London, 1905.
MORTON, A. L. (ed.), *The Political Writings of William Morris*, London, 1979.
MUTHESIUS, Hermann, *The English House*, (English Edition) London, 1979.
NAYLOR, Gillian, *The Arts and Crafts Movement: A Study of its Sources, Ideals and Influence on Design Theory*, London, 1981.
NAYLOR, Gillian, *The Bauhaus Reassessed: Sources and Design Theory*, London, 1985.
NEUMANN, E., *Bauhaus and Bauhaus People*, New York, 1970.

PEVSNER, Nikolaus, *Pioneers of the Modern Movement, from William Morris to Walter Gropius*, London, 1977.
READ, Herbert, *Art and Industry*, London, 1934.
R.I.B.A., *Architects of the Arts and Crafts Movement*, London 1983.
ROTH, L. M., *America Builds*, New York, 1983.
SCULLY, V., *The Shingle Style*, New Haven, 1955.
SMALL, Ian (ed.), *The Aesthetes*, London, 1979.
SOLOMON, Maynard, *Marxism and Art*, Brighton, 1979.
SPENCER, Isobel, *Walter Crane*, London, 1975.
SPENCER, Robin, *The Aesthetic Movement*, London, 1972.
STANSKY, Peter, *William Morris*, Oxford, 1983.
STEIN, R. B., *John Ruskin and Aesthetic Thought in America 1840–1900*, Harvard, 1967.
TATE GALLERY, *The Pre-Raphaelites*, (Exhibition Catalogue), London, 1984.
THOMPSON, E. P., *William Morris, Romantic to Revolutionary* London, 1976.
VALLANCE, Aymer, *The Life and Work of William Morris* New York, 1986.
WATKINSON, R., *Pre-Raphaelite Art and Design*, London 1970.
WHITFORD, Frank, *Bauhaus*, London, 1984.
WILLIAMS, Raymond, *Culture and Society 1780– 1950* Harmondsworth, 1979.
WRIGHT, Frank Lloyd, *The Arts and Crafts of the Machine* Princeton, 1930.

PICTURE CREDITS

Key: *t*=top; *b*=bottom; *l*=left; *r*=right; *c*=centre.

AMERICAN MUSEUM IN BRITAIN/(PHOTOS: DEREK BALMER): pp 24, 81. ARCHITECTURAL ASSOCIATION: pp 63, 72 *b*, 90 *b*, 110/111, 119. ASHMOLEAN MUSEUM, OXFORD: pp 30/31. BAUHAUS ARCHIV: pp 109, 123 *c*. BRIDGEMAN ART LIBRARY: pp 32, 37 (Victoria & Albert), 40/41, 44 *t* (V & A), 55 *b* (V & A), 58 (V & A), 61 (William Morris Gallery), 70 *l* (V & A), 78 (Bethnal Green Museum), 94 (V & A), 101 (Glasgow University), 123 *b* (V & A), 124 (Fine Art Society). EMMET BRIGHT: 89, 90 *t*, 91 *t*. BROOKLYN MUSEUM, NEW YORK: p 36. RICHARD BRYANT: pp 52/53. © PETER CORMACK: p 39. CORNING MUSEUM OF GLASS, CORNING, NY: p 77 *b*. PAINTON COWAN: pp 42 *t l*, 43 *b*. DESIGN COUNCIL: pp 48 *l*, 69 *b*, 122, 122/123, 125 *r*, 121 *t c*. E T ARCHIVE: pp 14/15 (Museum of London *t*), 18/19 (Victoria & Albert), 33 (Tate Gallery), 48/49 (V & A), 50 (William Morris Gallery), 61 *t l*, 65, 66, 72/73, 88, 96/97 (V & A), 98 *t r* (Dyson Perrins Museum), 99, 102/103, 125 *l* (V & A). FISHER FINE ART: pp 116/117, 117 *t*. © CLIVE HICKS: pp 42 *b l*, 93, 103, 104 *r*, 118/119. HIGH MUSEUM OF ART, ATLANTA, GEORGIA: pp 79, 80, 82, 83 *t*. ANGELO HORNAK: pp 11, 17, 44 *b*, (V & A), 45 (V & A), 59, 73 *b*, 91 *b*, 98 *b*, 112/113, 114, 116, 117 *b*, 121 *b*. JOHN JESSE & IRINA LASKI: pp 70 *r*, 98 *t l*. A F KERSTING: pp 34/35, 50/51, 54/55, 104 *l*, 106/107, 124/125 *t*. THE MANSELL COLLECTION: pp 7, 8, 10. © WILLIAM MORRIS GALLERY, LONDON: pp 60/61. DAVID O'CONNOR: pp 42 *t r*, 43 *t*. © RIBA/(PHOTOS: GEREMY BUTLER): pp 57, 62, 64, 68/69, 71. ROYAL SCHOOL OF NEEDLEWORK, LONDON: p 76. SANDERSONS: pp 46, 47. THE TATE GALLERY, LONDON: pp 27, 28/29. ED TEITELMAN: pp 20, 21 *b*, 22, 23, 25. MARK TWAIN MEMORIAL, HARTFORD, CT: p 77 *t*. VICTORIA & ALBERT MUSEUM, LONDON/(PHOTOS: EILEEN TWEEDY): pp 13, 16, 21 *t*, 52, 55 *t c*, 61 *t r*, 69 *t*, 72 *t*, 74, 83 *b*, 84, 85, 87 *t*, 95, 96, 97, 100, 105, 120, 123 *t*, 124/125 *b*.

126

INDEX